The Education of the Poor

Routledge Library in the History of Education

General Editor: Brian Simon,
Professor of Education, University of Leicester

The Education of the Poor

The history of a National
school 1824–1974

PAMELA SILVER

and

HAROLD SILVER

Routledge & Kegan Paul

London and Boston

First published in 1974
by Routledge & Kegan Paul Ltd
Broadway House, 68–74 Carter Lane,
London EC4V 5EL and
9 Park Street,
Boston, Mass. 02108, U.S.A.
Printed in Great Britain by
Willmer Brothers Limited, Birkenhead
and set in Modern Ext. No. 7

ISBN 0 7100 7804 8

Library of Congress Catalog Card No. 73–91036

Contents

To Claire and Vicki

General editor's preface

There are many histories of public – and endowed grammar – schools, well over 500. Indeed some schools, such as Eton and Rugby, have several historical volumes devoted to them. But from at least the early nineteenth century the vast majority of children did not attend these schools. They attended the elementary schools which originated with the Lancasterian Society, to be followed shortly after by those founded in connection with the National Society, the object of which was to promote 'The Education of the Poor in the Principles of the Established Church throughout England and Wales'. After 1870, of course, many attended the new board schools.

Literally thousands of elementary schools were founded during the nineteenth century, yet there is scarcely a published history of a single one of them. This volume is a history of precisely such a school; in this case an elementary school set up under the auspices of the National Society early in the nineteenth century. In so far as the school was established at Lambeth, and with prestigious support, it may not be altogether typical (in its foundation) of the great mass of National schools. Yet it has a continuous existence from 1824 to the present day, and, in general, this indicates that it was probably typical of the better organised National schools throughout this period.

The authors have found it possible to reconstruct the history of the school through the abundant records which have, unusually, survived. They are able to trace its development in the light both of the school's changing social context, and of changes in the national system of education. In this way this book, though a unique case history of a particular school, throws light on national developments in education in a way that general textbook histories cannot possibly achieve. It makes an unusual and welcome contribution to our understanding of educational change, and of the nature of the education offered to the people in the nineteenth century – and, indeed, right up to today.

BRIAN SIMON

Preface

Records of the life of schools for the children of the poor in the early nineteenth century are rare and fragmentary. It is not uncommon for schools to possess log books dating back to their first introduction in 1863, or for former Board schools to have these and other records dating from after 1870. St Mark's voluntary aided primary school is unusual in two respects: it has preserved an extensive collection of records dating back to its foundation as the Kennington National Schools, Lambeth, in South London, in 1824, and it still occupies the same premises. The invaluable feature of this collection of documents is that it gives details of some aspects of the school in the early decades of its existence, and makes it possible to trace a more or less unbroken story from then to the present day. The most comprehensive picture of the life of the school can be built up, of course, from 1863, when the headteachers began to keep their log book accounts of the day-to-day activities of the school.

This account of the school is concerned mainly with the nineteenth century, but a final chapter summarises its history in the twentieth century. The book is based mainly on the school's manuscript collection, supplemented from other sources where this has been possible and desirable. Miss E. M. Lewis, Correspondent to the managers, kindly lent us material in her possession. To Mr G. W. Lihou, headmaster of the school, and to the Rev. C. J. F. Scott, former chairman of the school managers, we are grateful for permission to use and publish information in the school's records. Without Mr Lihou's ready and constant help the book could not have been written, and we are grateful to him, to Mrs J. Tiller, the school secretary, and to Mr J. Fleming, the schoolkeeper, for their help and forbearance over a long period of time.

To Miss M. Y. Williams, archivist, and her staff at the Minet Library, Lambeth, we are extremely grateful for help in tracing information of various kinds. We have had valuable help also from Mr A. R. Neate, Record Keeper at the Greater London

Record Office, and from the staffs of the National Society and Lambeth Palace library. Mrs O. Wood and Mrs J. King of Rachel McMillan College both provided Pamela Silver with much appreciated advice and encouragement at an early stage in the evolution of this account. We are grateful to Professor Brian Simon and Mr Richard Luker for helpful comments on drafts of the book. No one apart from ourselves, however, bears any responsibility for what we have made of the material.

So much information is drawn from original sources that it would have been excessive to provide individual, detailed references on all occasions. It is hoped, however, that the summary indication of these sources at the beginning of the notes for each chapter will make it possible for anyone wishing to pursue the details further to do so without difficulty. A complete list of the records in the possession of the school (and not still in use) is given in the Bibliography. Full references to secondary material are, of course, given throughout and in the Bibliography. Spelling and the nineteenth-century use of capital letters have been largely modernised. For readers who may wish to pursue further some aspects of education opened up by this account there are suggestions in the section, Further reading.

The Attention of the Inhabitants of KENNINGTON is
respectfully solicited to

THE DISTRICT SCHOOLS

WHICH HAVE BEEN ERECTED IN THE

KENNINGTON OVAL,

IN WHICH NEARLY

FOUR HUNDRED CHILDREN

ARE RECEIVING

THE BLESSINGS OF A RELIGIOUS AND USEFUL EDUCATION.

THE Object in forming Establishments of this nature, which now happily exist in almost every Parish and District throughout the Kingdom, is, to train the Infant Poor to good and orderly habits, —to instil into their minds an early knowledge of their civil and religious duties,—to guard them, as far as possible, from the seductions of vice,—and to afford them the means of becoming good Christians, as well as useful and industrious Members of Society:—These are the benefits proposed by the Promoters of these Schools; benefits, it is presumed, not more essential to the Children themselves, and their Parents, than to the Community at large.

With this view, the Kennington Schools have been founded;— proper Regulations have been laid down for the management of them; the Instruction of the Children is conducted upon the approved National system;—and they regularly attend Divine Service at St. Mark's Church on each Sunday:—To these, suitable Admonitions are added for the observance of the Parents, without whose co-operation and good example, the Lessons inculcated at the Schools would, in too many cases, fail to produce the effects desired.

In the Girls' School, the afternoon of each day is devoted to the Instruction of the Children in plain Needle-work; and the Sums, which have been already received for the work done for Families in the Neighbourhood, have enabled the Committee to furnish certain Articles of Clothing to Forty Girls, whose Industry and good Conduct have been such as to deserve Encouragement, and whose Parents have been grateful for the benefits conferred on their Children.

The completion of the Buildings necessary for placing these Schools on an efficient and permanent footing, has occasioned a considerable expense in their first formation; and it is confidently hoped that in a District like that of Kennington, where an Establishment of this kind is manifestly requisite, the Inhabitants will kindly contribute their aid and support towards maintaining it.

The Subscribers are invited to visit the Schools occasionally, in order to satisfy themselves that they are so conducted as to merit their support.

August, 1828.

Chapter one

Social change and the education of the poor to 1820

Two schools, one for boys and one for girls, were opened in Kennington, at the Oval, in the parish of St Mary Lambeth, London, in November 1824 and March 1825 respectively. Like all schools of the period they were built by voluntary initiative on the basis of voluntary funds. They were connected with the Church of England and with one of the bodies which was concerned with the provision of popular education – the Church of England's National Society. The schools were intended for what the initial appeal for subscriptions described as 'the instruction of the infant poor'. It was proposed, explained this appeal, 'that the school shall be called "the Kennington and South Lambeth National School;" – that the children shall be taught strictly on the National plan, and regularly attend divine service at the new church at Kennington'. The schools were commonly referred to as National schools or District schools; they were also called the Oval schools, or – as the eighteenth-century schools for the children of the poor had been called – charity schools.

The creation of the schools (or departments of the same school, as they became later in the century) reflected the problems of population, church and education in the late eighteenth and early nineteenth centuries. Population was increasing, and new residential areas were being established – including in Lambeth. The Church of England was trying to keep pace with changes in the distribution of the population, and the new St Mark's Church, Kennington, with accommodation for over two thousand people, was consecrated as part of this process in June 1824.[1] The National Society for Promoting the Education of the Poor in the Principles of the Established Church was founded in 1811, as part of the growing effort to provide, through education, a means of dealing with some of the social problems associated with the industrial and urban developments already under way at the opening of the nineteenth century. The new

Kennington Schools, therefore, were the outcome of important social changes, the extent of which was clear to those who were involved in the debates about education. The impact of these changes is visible in the nervousness with which much of the debate was conducted. The early industrial and urban developments were accompanied by considerable confusion about the problems they created. There were profound conflicts about the desirability of educating the poor, and much opposition was expressed to the creation of schools. The question of how to tackle the increasingly acute new social problems was never more urgently discussed than in the decade preceding the foundation of the Kennington Schools, the decade following the end of the Napoleonic wars in 1815. War was followed by a period of economic dislocation, social tensions, and widespread popular protests and political and social conflict. A sermon which gives a clear indication of current attitudes to education, against this background of social change, was one preached by the Rev. J. T. Allen in Manchester in 1819. Allen's purpose in the sermon was to argue against opponents of the provision of education for the children of the poor. He did this within a historical framework, reminding his listeners that 'within the space of the last half century, the whole frame and mechanism of society, in every large and commercial district, has undergone a thorough and most material change'. Commerce and manufacture had 'essentially changed' the character of society at all levels, and created problems of a new dimension. Among the wealthier sections of society:[2]

> The simple manners, and the frugal fare, which had hitherto prevailed, were succeeded by habits of luxury and refinement in diet and in dress. The population of the town was no longer confined to the number of its native inhabitants, but large multitudes of strangers were drawn together from distant places, for the purpose of traffic, or in search of employment and subsistence . . . In a large and crowded manufactory, it was impossible for the master to exercise the same patriarchal influence and authority over the moral character and conduct of those who were in his employ . . . Such was the general corruption of manners which resulted from the sudden and important change which took place in the circumstances of society, – such are the baneful diseases

which are universally found to accompany the growth of national prosperity, where they are not timely prevented by wise and vigorous remedies.

The sermon was intended to prove that the spirit of disaffection which many people saw and feared among the 'lower orders of society' was the result not of education but of these changes in the structure of society. Lambeth, as we shall see, had its share of 'multitudes of strangers', manufactories, sudden changes and 'corruption of manners'. Nationally, education came to be seen by some people as one of the 'wise and vigorous remedies' necessary for a society that had undergone the disruptions attendant upon industrialisation on a scale, at a rate and with a sustained momentum not previously known in history. The educational response to these changes in 'the whole frame and mechanism of society' was slow, limited, patchy and organised on a purely voluntary basis.

There had, of course, been schools, educational ideas and proposals, and educational initiatives of many kinds in the eighteenth century. England and Wales had a long established network of endowed grammar schools, many of which provided what came to be called 'elementary' education for the younger children, as well as or instead of the classical curriculum which was their main purpose. At an elementary level there were also some endowed parish schools, 'private-venture' and dame schools – varying in their stability, standards and distribution. Generally speaking, however, the formal education of poor children in pre-industrial, eighteenth-century England was seen by the majority of people as unnecessary. The charity schools created from the beginning of the eighteenth century for the children of the poor, reached a relatively small proportion of this class of the community, and were very unevenly spread over the country; they were viewed, nevertheless, with a certain suspicion or hostility in many quarters. Charity schools provided a basic education in reading and arithmetic, sometimes writing and often relevant practical crafts and skills appropriate to the likely future occupations of the children. All of this was provided within a framework of moral and religious education and worship; children were put into uniform and taught the ways of obedience. A summary of the purpose of Derbyshire charity schools as they still were in the early nineteenth century, indicates that:[3]

Moral and religious instruction took a large share of the
curriculum. Indeed, indoctrination of the principles of the
Church of England was frequently the main object of the
endowments: 'instructing and educating the children there
in piety, virtue and good literature', 'to teach them their
duty to God and man', 'catechism, liturgy and the principles
of the Church of England . . .', 'to teach poor children to
read and write and that the schoolmaster should attend to
morals'.

Some charitable school foundations took the form of 'schools
of industry', where the element of preparation for employment
was dominant. Basket-making, spinning, shirt-making, or other
activities related to the locality formed the central part of the
curriculum, products were sold, and the children sometimes
received cash benefits when profits were made. Activities
designed to train boys and girls for future employment as
servants were the most common, and some supporting education
was normally provided in the basic skills and religious and
moral training. Where workhouses appointed teachers, the
model of the industrial school was also frequently followed.

Charity schools, sometimes endowed but invariably supported
by subscriptions, were seen by some critics – in the changing
circumstances of the late eighteenth century – to be inadequate
as a means of approaching the problem of the newly growing
towns, and of providing education on a wide enough scale. At
the beginning of the nineteenth century Sir Thomas Bernard
described the charity schools as being 'insufficient', lacking in
adequate financial support, and too expensive to run. In many
schools indeed the numbers had been deliberately reduced, and
the Society for Promoting Christian Knowledge – the body
which had sponsored the schools since 1699 – had explained
that they 'thought fit to lessen the number of children taught in
them, that the rest may be entirely supported; which is the
reason, the number now taught is short of what it was formerly'.
This, considered Bernard, was a process which led to patronage
of a few children, whereas the real question was 'how the most
extensive and permanent good can be done'.[4]

The general position, therefore, at the beginning of the
nineteenth century, was that restricted school provision was
available to the children of the poor in some areas, and that the

form which such provision took was beginning to be considered
expensive and inadequate to the needs of the areas of growing
population and concentrated social problems. An attempt to
contribute to the solution of this set of problems was made in
the 1780s in the form of the Sunday school movement. The
Sunday schools were aimed at the children who were either
employed in industry during the week or were left to maraud
in the streets, in both cases normally without any form of
schooling. If, as with the charity schools, the intention was also
primarily a religious and moral one, the Sunday schools were
much more of a mass phenomenon and provided a wider basis
of rudimentary literacy, on the basis of which many working
men in the early nineteenth century managed with difficulty
to build a self-acquired education. The Sunday schools were
the first attempt to fashion a mass education adjusted to the
conditions of the changing society.

In the decades following the onset of industrialisation, the
French revolution, the Napoleonic wars and an unprecedented
growth in English towns, the provision of day schools for the
children of the poor – as at Kennington – was not something
which happened automatically, without effort or without
opposition. The charity schools had been criticised as risking
to give poor children ideas above their proper station in life;
Sunday schools were attacked, especially after the French
revolution, as being subversive and undermining the authority
of the Church. When, in the early nineteenth century, Church
and Dissent both set to work to provide schools through the
National and British Societies, there was fresh opposition, as
there was to any scheme to involve the state in the provision of
education. Popular education was attacked vociferously in the
mid-1790s, when, under the impact of events in France, a 'wave
of panic poisoned the minds of the governing classes'.[5] Sir
Thomas Bernard described how the Society for Bettering the
Condition of the Poor was founded at a time when 'the horrors
of the French Revolution had renewed the prejudices against
any general system of education. Many candid and enlightened
men – men who would not have withheld any good thing from
the poor, then apprehended danger from a general diffusion
even of the elementary knowledge of reading and writing.'
There were, he wrote in 1812, 'still some pious and conscientious
persons adverse to the extension of instruction to the poor,

B

beyond reading merely: and one of the labours of the Society has been, to remove these prejudices.'[6]

Prejudice was strengthened in many quarters by the radical developments of the 1810s. Luddism at the beginning of the decade was followed by the growth of popular radicalism after the end of the Napoleonic wars in 1815. William Cobbett's *Political Register*, the Hampden Clubs, attempts at insurrection, Peterloo – these are representative features of the second half of the 1810s. It is easy to see, therefore, why the Rev. J. T. Allen opened his 1819 sermon with the remarks:

> The spirit of insubordination and disaffection which has so unhappily prevailed of late amongst the lower orders of society, in addition to other more immediate and alarming evils, has certainly been productive of this great mischief: – It has strengthened and confirmed the prejudices, which many well-meaning persons have all along entertained, as to the policy and propriety of those exertions which have been made for the education of the children of the poor.

There were people, he continued, who had 'always beheld every system of national education with jealousy and distrust'. He had been frequently compelled to listen to 'weak and idle calumnies' against education, and 'to vindicate the cause of national education against the obstinate prejudices of its avowed adversaries'.[7]

The educational movement of which the Kennington schools were a product took shape, therefore, in a situation such as this, with unparalleled social changes taking place, and new towns and districts growing without any of the ties of squire and church that had been typical of the small agricultural community, and the old market town. The pastoral role of the church had been weakened or destroyed by the changes, and the church had few or no footholds in large areas where population concentrated round new industrial developments, and in major commercial centres and ports, including, of course, London. The education movement sponsored mainly by the churches at the beginning of the nineteenth century was built on a sense of urgency in the face of social and political danger. The National Society was created, in its own words, with:[8]

the sole object in view being to communicate to the poor

generally, by the means of a summary mode of education,
lately brought into practice, such knowledge and habits, as
are sufficient to guide them through life, in their proper
stations, especially to teach the doctrines of Religion,
according to the principles of the Established Church, and
to train them to the performance of their religious duties by
early discipline.

The early nineteenth-century education movement contained
people who advocated schooling on humanitarian and philanthropic grounds, as a right, and for other reasons. In the puzzling
new world of the early industrial revolution most of them
considered that the children of the poor needed, unlike their
eighteenth-century predecessors, to be 'guided through life' by
schools. The aim of the educators was in general limited, in the
National Society's words, to teaching the children of the poor
'sufficient', to influencing their behaviour without raising their
aspirations beyond 'their proper stations'.

The movement which was to dominate English popular
education for the first half of the nineteenth century was that
based on the monitorial school. Both Joseph Lancaster, founder
of the largely nonconformist British Society, and Andrew Bell,
father of the Church of England's National Society, evolved at
about the same time the idea and practice of teaching more
children more cheaply (and, it was believed, more efficiently)
by using monitors, older children, to teach younger ones.
Lancaster was faced, when he began a school in his father's
house in Southwark in 1798, with the 'perplexity how to provide
sufficient teachers', and he 'according to his friends, invented,
or, according to his enemies, derived from Dr. Bell, the plan of
teaching younger children by the elder. This – the monitorial –
plan attracted much attention; its simplicity and economy
procured for it extensive favour.'[9] Lancaster's scheme in the
Borough Road, Southwark, and described in his *Improvements
in Education* in 1806, was the stimulus behind the monitorial
movement as developed by both Church and Dissent, and until
the Church of England set up its own society Lancaster had
support from some churchmen, aristocracy and royalty, as
well as from nonconformist circles. A description of the Borough
Road school in 1804 indicated the extent of the reliance on
monitors by the single master in charge of the school, which

was at that moment 500 strong, and was preparing to take another 200:

> The system of tuition is almost entirely conducted by the boys . . . the school is divided into classes; to each of these a lad is appointed as monitor. He is responsible for the morals, improvement, good order, and cleanliness of the whole class . . . If a lad in one class becomes qualified for removal to a higher, he receives an appropriate reward, and his monitor also a similar one.

An important feature of Lancaster's system and of monitorial schools generally was the extensive use of rewards and punishments, and Lancaster's monitors were responsible, for example, for distributing 'orders of merit', on the basis of which prizes such as balls, kites and sums of money were given. There were monitors in general charge of, for example, cleanliness or slates: 'every duty has its respective officer, and the fidelity and assiduity displayed in their discharge is surprising.'[10] This new kind of schooling, it has been said, 'was not unlike the new factory both in appearance and in method, the definite rewards and punishments of the one corresponding to the wages and fines of the other.'[11] Both factory and school, in their scale and methods of operation, represented profound changes in English social organisation, a fact which did not go unnoticed by contemporaries:[12]

> The man who first made a practical use of the division of labour, gave a new power to the application of corporal strength, and simplified and facilitated the most irksome and laborious operations . . . But that man, whatever was his merit, did not more essential service to mechanical, than Dr. Bell has done to intellectual operations. It is the division of labour in his schools, that leaves the master the easy task of directing the movements of the whole machine, instead of toiling ineffectually at a single part.

It was in 1797 that Dr Andrew Bell, an Anglican clergyman, described in *An Experiment in Education* a new system of school organisation with which he had experimented in Madras, and which in its use of the 'mutual' or 'monitorial' (or, as it came to be known also, the 'Madras') system, was very similar to that adopted by Lancaster. The enthusiasm for Lancaster's work led to the creation of the Royal Lancasterian Society in 1808, and in 1814 this became the British and Foreign School Society. In opposition to this undenominational body and its schools, the Church of England set up the National Society in 1811. In discussing the foundation of the Society its main historian, H. J. Burgess, has made the point that 'Lancaster and his friends forestalled Bell by four years', but that it was 'not true that the action of Churchmen in founding their own society was simply a riposte to the Dissenters. On the contrary, the clergy had been active in founding parish schools even before the end of the eighteenth century.'[13] That the Church of England had been involved in earlier educational efforts is, of course, true. It is also true, however, that the Church of England was responding in 1811 to the successful new initiative sponsored mainly by nonconformists in an entirely new social situation. The Church was unwilling to allow the emergence of a system of popular education over which it did not exercise control. Burgess has described the creation of the Society in 1811, with a committee which 'for many years remained a High Church preserve', at a founding meeting which resolved 'that the national religion should be made the foundation of national education and should be the first and chief thing taught to the poor, according to the excellent liturgy and catechism provided by our Church'. He concluded that 'a limited secular instruction based upon the monitorial system and joined to a dogmatic and disciplinary religious education was the original objective of the founders of the National Society.'[14] Elsewhere he quotes a letter from the *Gentleman's Magazine* in 1811, which asserted that 'to inform the ignorant and to save the souls of millions of the human race, is the end of the National Society'.[15]

Bell's methods, adopted rigidly by the National Society and the schools associated with it, consisted of the use of monitors (normally called 'teachers' and 'assistants' in National schools), and relentless repetition of the material: 'In Dr. Bell's schools, if so many as three mistakes, however trivial, are made in the course of the hearing, the class is ordered back again to learn and relearn it . . . The books which Dr. Bell's scholars learn, they go through a second, and sometimes even a third time.'[16] The master taught the monitors, the monitors taught the 'classes' – groups of children who were all, it should be remembered, in a single large room. Within the groups most of the work was rote learning and recitation of lessons in unison, including the repetition of monosyllables and combinations of syllables graded by difficulty, as the basic means of learning spelling and reading ('these elaborate methods for destroying meaning', says one writer, 'were held to be a virtue').[17] Some of the work was done in pairs, as at the National Society's central school at Baldwin's Gardens, in London:[18]

> when the lesson has been read, the members of the class, in succession, question one another on its meaning. Here each child is tutor and pupil in turn, and the incitement of emulation operates as well in the art of questioning as of answering. The teacher and assistant act as umpires, taking care that no fit questions are omitted, and no unfitting ones asked: and correcting or supplying the answers wherever necessary. By these means all the children of a class are qualified to become teachers.

These kinds of methods, this kind of organisation, account for the speed with which the system was adopted. The aims were clear and plausible. The cost of providing only one adult teacher to supervise large numbers of children, and the simplicity of the materials and methods, were attractive to a society looking for easy, cheap solutions. The diocesan organisation for the establishment of schools in Durham declared in 1818 that it aimed to disseminate 'among the children of the poor that system of instruction, of which the direct tendency is, and consequence may be, that they will be rescued from vice and error, and be made good Christians, and profitable members of the community', and that this 'is more and more becoming evident to the public'.[19] Lancaster himself had pointed out in 1806 that his system was not intended to infringe upon the established charity or parochial schools, 'but to provide for a class of children with which they are unconnected, and which they do not provide for at all'.[20] That the British and National Societies provided a simple solution to a problem in providing for this class of children had indeed become evident to the public by the time the National schools were founded in Kennington. The statistics are unreliable, but the order of magnitude they indicate is clear. The National Society's report for 1826, for example, summarises the position:[21]

In the 1st Annual Report of this Society, the Committee had
to state that there existed only about 40 schools in the
Kingdom on the National plan, containing altogether about
8000 children. In the report of this, their 15th year, they
have the satisfaction of mentioning the existence of about
2,200 National schools, in which not less than 330,000 poor
children are at this time receiving education.

In 1817 the National Society estimated that it had over 1,000
schools in union with it, with a total of some 155,000 children.
Two years later it estimated that there were nearly 1,500 schools
and over 200,000 children (though at both dates a substantial
proportion of these children attended only on Sundays). In
1829 the Society's returns indicated:

Sunday and daily attendance	boys	100,477
	girls	74,136
	total	174,613
Sunday only or additional	boys	51,089
	girls	51,547
	total	102,636

The committee also believed that the returns on which these
figures were based represented some two-thirds of the schools
actually in existence, and believed that the grand total was in
the region of 360,000.[22]

Although, as we shall see in the case of Lambeth, the British
Society made the earlier start, the greater resources and
parochial organisation which buttressed the National Society
soon gave it the dominant position. When, from 1833, government subsidies began to be available to the two societies for the
building of schools, the subsidies were distributed in proportion
to the money raised by the supporters of the two societies, and
it was the National Society that year by year received by far
the greater share.

We shall be looking in detail at the foundation and functioning
of two specific schools, but it is clear that the incentive to provide
schooling for 'the instruction of the infant poor' in a growing
district of South London was part of a national development.
The monitorial system had established itself as all-pervasive in
National and British schools, and it was also adopted in the

early nineteenth century by other schools, including factory
schools, and some grammar and public schools. The system
was built on a sense of confidence and optimism, the full extent
of which can be judged from the first report of the National
Society:[23]

> The facility of communicating instruction by the system
> now intended to be brought into general use; its efficiency
> in fixing the attention, and inculcating the things taught;
> the eagerness, and even delight, with which the children
> embrace it; the entire possession which it takes of their
> minds, so as to render them pliant and obedient to
> discipline . . . and the anxiety which their parents shew to
> have them instructed, are powerful instruments, both for
> infusing into their minds good knowledge, and forming
> them to good habits. The economy with which, after the
> first formation of proper schools, it may be conducted, is also
> such as to give us reason to hope, that the very lowest classes
> of society may receive the benefits of it, and that it may
> become universal.

Modern verdicts on the system have been harsh. A representative view is contained in the comment that 'he would be a bold
man who would defend on educational grounds the mutual
system of education as practised by either Bell or Lancaster . . .
Fundamentally the system was at fault in entrusting the real
business of education to child instructors and transforming the
adult teacher into a mere superintendent.'[24] Some caution is
necessary, however, in pronouncing judgment on the early
work of the National and British schools, partly because of the
lack of detailed sources which would enable us to see how the
system worked in practice across a range of schools. A national
system of inspection was not introduced until 1839 and it is
not easy to make judgments about the value of the system in
the early years of the century from evidence in the inspectors'
reports published from 1840. School log books were not required
to be kept until 1863. There are a number of accounts of schools
in the societies' reports, some autobiographies of people educated
at them, comments written by visitors and interested observers
and participants such as Sir Thomas Bernard, and a small
number of other sources. Most of the detail available relates to
well-known or model schools like Baldwin's Gardens, and there

is conflicting evidence as to how much children enjoyed or benefited from monitorial schooling. Generally speaking the societies and the local promoters of schools insisted on the strict implementation of their teaching schemes, as is clear from the intention of the promoters at Kennington to ensure 'that the children shall be taught strictly on the National plan'. In cases where teachers received a brief period of induction into the system they were instructed purely in its application as a piece of ready-made machinery. The National Society insisted that only religious tracts sold by the Society for Promoting Christian Knowledge should be allowed to be used in National schools. Yet, as the details of the Kennington Schools will show, this is not the entire story. Among other things, the size and position of schools, the abilities of the schoolmaster or mistress, and the attitudes of the influential figures among the school benefactors and managers, may have influenced the ways in which schools worked, even within a seemingly inflexible system. The content of the schemes as described by Bell and Lancaster, and the declared purposes of monitorial education, do of course indicate clearly enough the limitations of the system. The level of achievement in the schools was low. As a concept and in practice the monitorial system is open to every possible kind of criticism. The criticism must take into account, however, our lack of detailed information about schools, and the historical context within which the monitorial system was adopted – including the availability and credibility of alternative approaches to education.

There were, indeed, at the end of the eighteenth and in the early decades of the nineteenth centuries, radical educational views and experiments of various kinds, but rarely accepted widely as being applicable to the situation for which monitorial schools were evolved. The only real exception is the educational work of Robert Owen, mainly at New Lanark in the 1810s and early 1820s, from which stemmed an infant school movement, whose schools for younger children were supplementary to, and not designed to replace, the monitorial schools. If radical views about the content and processes of education failed to have any impact on mass schooling in the first half of the nineteenth century, neither did radical views about the provision of education other than through voluntary channels. Lancaster and Bell both argued strongly against the idea of compulsory schooling. Lancaster saw it as unacceptable to the Englishman, with his 'spirit, breathing the language of independence' and unwilling to accept the idea of compulsion: 'teachers or parents of any spirit will not bear attempts to reform them by force, however respectably sanctioned'.[25] Bell was aware that 'some ancient and military nations' had educated the youth 'at the public charge, and in a prescribed form'. In a free country, however, 'and in the improved state of commerce and the arts, this practice does not admit of being universally adopted, and if it did, would not be productive of general benefit'.[26]

The two societies worked to prevent each other from filling a vacuum wherever one existed. Although the British Society had some support outside nonconformist circles (for example, from secularists), the societies became identified with sectarian positions. These became explicit and militant as attempts to bring the state into the educational field began to grow and appeared, from their embattled positions, to favour one side or the other. State finance was not involved in the building of schools until 1833, and then to a limited extent. A state machinery of inspection was not created until 1839, and moves to finance a form of teacher training which would improve on the use of monitors were not made until 1846. The first national elementary education act did not follow until 1870. Up to that date the story of mass education for the children of the poor is entirely, and for the remainder of the century is to a considerable degree, one of rival societies, representing for the most part the nonconformist and Church of England communities.

Notes

N.B. Items in the collection of manuscripts and documents relating to the Kennington Schools are not referred to individually. At the beginning of the notes for each chapter the relevant sources for the history of the schools are listed, as for this chapter:

A bound volume of minutes and various other documents, printed and manuscript, 1823–40.

1 Survey of London, xxvi, *The Parish of St Mary Lambeth*, pt ii, general editor F. H. W. Sheppard, pp. 31–2.

2 J. T. Allen, *A Vindication of the Moral and Religious Instruction of the Children of the Poor*, pp. 5–9.

3 Marion Johnson, *Derbyshire Village Schools in the Nineteenth Century*, p. 21.

4 Thomas Bernard, Preface to *Of the Education of the Poor; being*

the first part of a digest of the
reports of the Society for Bettering
the Condition of the Poor (London,
1809), pp. 12–14.
5 Frank Smith, *A History of English
Elementary Education 1760–1902*,
p. 58.
6 Thomas Bernard, *The Barrington
School* (London, 1812), pp. 5–7.
7 Allen, *Vindication*, pp. 1–3.
8 *First Annual Report of the
National Society* (London, 1812),
p. 18.
9 Horace Mann, *Census of Great
Britain, 1851: Education in Great
Britain*, pp. xv–xvi.
10 *Of the Education of the Poor*,
pp. 159–61.
11 Smith, *History of English
Elementary Education*, p. 75.
12 Bernard, Preface to *Of the
Education of the Poor*, pp. 35–6.
13 H. J. Burgess and P. A. Welsby,
*A Short History of the National
Society 1811–1961*, p. 3.
14 Henry James Burgess, *Enterprise
in Education*, pp. 22–4.
15 H. J. Burgess, 'The Educational
History of the National Society

1811–1833', p. 32.
16 Bernard, Preface to *Of the
Education of the Poor*, pp. 23–4.
17 Mary Sturt, *The Education of the
People*, p. 32.
18 *Seventh Annual Report of the
Society for the Encouragement of
Parochial Schools in the Diocese of
Durham and Hexhamshire* (Newcastle upon Tyne, 1818), p. 15.
19 *Ibid.*, p. 14.
20 Joseph Lancaster, *An Appeal for
Justice in the Cause of Ten
Thousand Poor Children* (3rd edn
1807), p. 40.
21 *Fifteenth Annual Report of the
National Society* (London, 1826),
p. 10.
22 Burgess, 'Educational History of
the National Society', p. 155.
23 *First Annual Report of the
National Society*, pp. 18–19.
24 Burgess, 'Educational History of
the National Society', p. 230.
25 Joseph Lancaster, *Improvements
in Education*, pp. 182–3.
26 Andrew Bell, *The Madras School*,
p. 290.

Chapter two

The Kennington National Schools

Lambeth was a rapidly growing district of London in the early decades of the nineteenth century. Even in the eighteenth century the parish had been assuming greater importance. The riverside employments in the northern part of Lambeth were supplemented by an increase in market gardening, especially when easier communication with central London became possible after the completion of Westminster Bridge in 1751. As a result of the opening of the bridge 'the builders set to work and Kennington became a suburb of London'.[1] For the remainder of the eighteenth century, however, this suburb remained, as did Lambeth as a whole, sparsely populated by comparison with London north of the Thames. Of Lambeth's 4,000 acres, in the period immediately prior to the foundation of the Kennington Schools, more than half consisted of land under the plough, meadow, pasture, market garden, nursery, commons or woodland. Wharfs and timber-yards accounted for twenty acres, 'manufactories' for 100 acres, and the remainder was covered mostly by houses, buildings, roads and private gardens. Just as market gardens had replaced fields, however, so buildings now began to replace both. At the end of the eighteenth century there were some 250 acres of market gardens, but in the first two decades of the new century the increase in building had reduced the figure to eighty. By the time the Kennington Schools were opened, however, there were still 630 acres of meadowland and 730 acres of arable and pasture land in Lambeth.[2] A description of the appointment of the first organist of St Mark's Church explains that he 'lived in a house near the Oval Schools; it was then a very lonely spot . . . The Oval was a lonely place, and not many persons passed that way.' The Oval itself, it was said in 1826, was 'a beautiful nursery ground of an oval form . . . This spot is peculiarly delightful, the sides of the road, for some distance, being formed by this nursery ground, and a fine plantation laid out to resemble a park.'[3]

How rapidly the district was growing is clear from the population and housing figures. There were some 5,000 inhabited houses in the parish in 1800, 7,704 in 1811 and 9,294 in 1821. Between the latter two dates the total population of the parish increased from 41,644 to 57,638 (it had been just under 28,000 at the time of the first national census in 1801). The population of England and Wales, which had been steadily rising in the second half of the eighteenth century, increased from approximately ten to twelve million in the same decade. The population of London rose from some 1,100,000 to 1,226,000 at the same time.[4] The country's population increase was being concentrated mainly in the new industrial towns of the North and in the capital.

The expansion of the South London suburbs was stimulated especially by the opening of the new bridges at Vauxhall (in 1816) and Waterloo (in 1817). Vauxhall Bridge was of direct importance to Kennington, and its opening was responsible for the creation of Harleyford Road, in which the new National schools were soon to be founded. A description of changes following the opening of the bridge emphasises the effect on housing conditions:[5]

> the adjacent parts of Kennington were built over and shut off from the fields so that as a residential neighbourhood Kennington began slowly but surely to deteriorate. Poorer and less 'desirable tenants' occupied the houses and Kennington became a mean and despised suburb. The leaseholders naturally wished to keep their revenues at high water mark and overcrowding was the consequence . . . Houses of 10 rooms frequently sheltered 8 families, necessary repairs were not carried out and a period of gloom and decay followed.

The discrepancy between this picture and that of the 'lonely spot' at the Oval emphasises that at this point in urban growth new concentrations of population were in pockets, and not distributed evenly over what was still a substantially rural district. Housing was still mainly following the developing pattern of roads, and the opening of Waterloo Bridge, to the north, was having the same effect, leading to the[6]

> rapid filling in of Lambeth Marsh and St George's Fields with terraces of good late Georgian and Regency houses and also to the building of rows of small houses near the river. Moreover, building was taking place along the main roads to Camberwell Green and Kennington Church – ribbon development only, leaving the intervening spaces to be filled in later.

In addition to agricultural and riverside pursuits in the parish, the new population found other trades and occupations. There were already brick works, and new industries included the manufacture of glass and pottery, printing works, and on the east side of Kennington Common, a vitriol works which was to be a major source of local pollution for decades. The South London Waterworks was opened between Kennington Lane and the Oval in 1807. Industries such as these, and other trades which accompanied the expansion of the suburban community, resulted in an increase in the number of families engaged chiefly in trades and manufactures, as measured in the census returns, from 4,491 to 6,969 between 1811 and 1821. The extent to which this dimension of social change brought with it substantial problems is reflected in the Poor Law statistics. In the first eighteen years of the nineteenth century the total annual poor rate raised in Lambeth increased from £11,691 to £47,870; the numbers in the workhouse rose from 431 to 1,250 and the number on outdoor relief rose from 347 to 1,867.[7] An argument commonly used in the early decades of the nineteenth century was that education was a necessary and cheap means of reducing pauperism and crime.

The problems of an expanding and more mobile population created difficulties for the Church of England, based on a parochial structure that was ill-equipped to cope with the new urban communities – even where the Church was vigorous enough to make the attempt. One outcome of the Napoleonic wars was the vote by parliament in 1818 of a million pounds (another half a million was later added) to build churches in areas where population had recently expanded. This was intended as a 'great demonstration to Almighty God for the

return of peace'.[8] The grants were to be administered by a
Church Building Commission: four such 'Commissioners'' or
'Waterloo' churches were built in Lambeth, one of them being
St Mark's, Kennington, the building of which began in 1822
and which was completed two years later. In 1824 the parish
of Lambeth was split into ecclesiastical districts in order to
take account of the new realities of the parish; it was with this
development in mind, as well as the trends in the parish generally,
that the appeal on behalf of the Kennington Schools was made
in 1823:

> considering the great extent of the Parish of Lambeth, its
> rapidly increasing population, and its expected division into
> ecclesiastical districts, it is highly expedient that steps
> should be promptly taken for establishing new schools in
> suitable parts of the parish. The Kennington district appeared
> to present the first claim.

The opening of the new church and the foundation of the schools
were parallel and related developments. The problems of the
new urban districts were widely seen, in fact, as joint problems
of religion and education. The National Society, like the British
and Foreign School Society, had come into existence, as we
have seen, to try to solve some of the problems of towns in
which the population had lost many of their traditional sign-
posts.

There was no doubt in the minds of those active in the two
societies that the problem of education was an extremely
urgent one. In 1817 British Society supporters in Lambeth
appealed for help with the establishment of schools 'without
regarding the religious opinions' of parents. An 'Address to
the Inhabitants of Lambeth' emphasised the extent of the
problem:

> Considerable pains have been taken to ascertain the state
> of the poor, as to education, in the parish of Lambeth . . .
> By a personal inquiry recently made in a small part of the
> parish, it was found, that out of forty-one families, com-
> prising one hundred and twenty-four children between the
> ages of six and fourteen, there were only twenty-six who

received daily instruction; thirty that occasionally attended Sunday Schools; whilst the remaining seventy were wholly without education. In another part, comprising three hundred and forty-one children between the ages of six and fourteen, two hundred and two were found to be uneducated.

In spite of ambiguities in this description (it is not clear, for example, whether 'uneducated' means not receiving education at that moment, or never having had any), the tone is one of urgency and matches other descriptions of illiteracy and the lack of education in rapidly growing towns and districts in the early decades of the nineteenth century.

It was against this background of national and local change, educational need and existing effort that the first moves towards the foundation of the Kennington Schools were made early in 1823.

There were schools of one kind or another already in existence in Lambeth before this date. The Licensed Victuallers' School, for example, had been opened in Kennington Lane in 1803. Archbishop Temple's Boys' School, then known as the Parochial Boys' School, had been formed in the middle of the eighteenth century from three existing foundations, and occupied a site at Lambeth Green, near Lambeth Palace. Archbishop Tenison's School for girls had been endowed in 1715, and in 1817 had united with a school supported by voluntary subscriptions to form 'an union on the national system'. In the early 1820s the funds of the Archbishop Tenison's foundation improved to an extent which enabled the trustees to donate £500 towards the Kennington Schools.[9] The British Society had succeeded in 1817 in establishing a school called the Lambeth Association School, and the existence of the British Society's 1817 appeal as a frontispiece to the Kennington Schools' first minute book may mean that the National Society's efforts were at least partly inspired, in Lambeth as elsewhere, by the challenge from the nonconformists.

A parochial school known as the Union School or Lambeth Girls' School had been established in Nine Elms, in the western part of the parish, to serve the poor children of Lambeth, Battersea and Clapham. This school was in cramped and unsatisfactory premises, and when the idea of building schools for boys and girls at Kennington was broached it was decided

to try to amalgamate the Nine Elms School and the Kennington Schools. There were objections, however, from supporters of the Nine Elms school who believed that it would, by moving, fail to provide education for its existing catchment area; since a house then became available in the immediate neighbourhood, 'eligible for carrying on the schools in a more effective manner', a local meeting resolved that it was 'expedient to continue the school in its present situation'. Mr Richard Cannon, of Upper Kennington Lane, who had been active in support of the Nine Elms school, became treasurer of the committee for the Kennington Schools. Cannon, described in the 1851 census as a 'clerk, Adjutant General's office',[10] was to hold the position of treasurer for thirty years, and it was thanks to his care that so many of the early records were collected together in a form which enabled them to be preserved.

The schooling provided at Kennington was to be free, and the committee, including the Rev. G. D'Oyly, Rector of Lambeth, and the Rev. W. Otter,[11] Minister of St Mark's Church, set about collecting funds to establish and maintain the new schools.

The largest donation came from the subscribers to the Lambeth parochial schools, who, it was recorded, 'have with great liberality, agreed to contribute from their funds the sum of £900 (£3 per cent Consuls) towards the erection of school rooms in the Kennington district'. £300 of this came from the boys' school in Lambeth Green, and £600 from the Lambeth Girls' School, both in April 1824. From the Archbishop Tenison foundation came, as we have seen, £500. King George IV donated £100. Few National schools can have started from such a substantial financial basis. Receipts recorded in the accounts of the school for the years 1824–6 read as shown in Table 1. Individual donations and subscriptions came from all over the parish, and, as the previous accounts show, loans were raised. In addition to the continuing search for donations a collection was held for the schools after a sermon in December 1824 and this became a regular biannual feature at St Mark's Church until 1835 (when it became annual). Sermons were also preached at the beginning in other churches in the locality, 'for the benefit of the National Schools, recently formed in the Kennington district'. Of the printed announcements of such sermons one of the earliest in the records was as follows:

KENNINGTON
National Schools.

ON SUNDAY NEXT,
The 19th November, 1826,
TWO SERMONS
WILL BE PREACHED IN
St. Mark's Church,
KENNINGTON.

THAT IN THE MORNING
By the Rev. WILLIAM OTTER, A.M.
Minister of St. Mark's, Kennington

THAT IN THE EVENING
By the Rev. WILLIAM EDWARDS, A.M.
Assistant Minister of St. Mark's, Kennington.

For the Benefit of the National Schools
RECENTLY FORMED IN THE
KENNINGTON DISTRICT.

Divine Service will begin at Eleven o'Clock in the Morning;
And at Half-past Six in the Evening.

APPROPRIATE PSALMS WILL BE SUNG
ON THE OCCASION.

N.B. The Friends and Supporters of Institutions of this Nature, which afford so many advantages to the Poor, are most earnestly invited to contribute their Aid to the National Schools recently erected in the Kennington Oval, in which nearly Four Hundred Children are now receiving the Blessings of a Religious and Useful Education.

In the Girls' School the afternoon of each day is devoted to the Instruction of the Children in plain Needle-work, and the Sum which has been already received for Work done for Families in the Neighbourhood, has enabled the Committee to furnish certain Articles of Clothing to Thirty Girls, whose Industry and good Conduct have been such as to deserve Encouragement, and whose Parents have been grateful for the benefits conferred on their Children.

The Completion of the Buildings necessary for placing these Schools on an efficient and permanent footing, has occasioned a considerable Expence in their first Formation,—for the defraying of which, as well as for the Annual Support of the Schools, the Committee very respectfully appeal to the Benevolence and Liberality of the Inhabitants of the District.

The Subscribers are invited to visit the Schools occasionally, in order to satisfy themselves that they are so conducted as to merit their Support.

Donations and Subscriptions will be very thankfully received by the Treasurer, Mr. CANNON, of No. 4, Upper Kennington Lane, Vauxhall; or by any of the Gentlemen of the Committee.

The churches were in general the focus of early financial effort in support of National schools. The machinery can be seen in a letter from the King in July 1823 to be read in churches in order to raise funds for the National Society. The King's letter urged[12]

that upon this occasion the Ministers in each parish do effectually excite their parishioners to a liberal contribution; whose benevolence towards carrying on the said charitable work, shall be collected the week following, at their respective dwellings, by the Churchwardens or Overseers of the Poor in each parish; and the Ministers of the several parishes are to cause the sums so collected, to be paid immediately to the Treasurer for the time being of the said Society, to be accounted for by him to the said Society, and applied to the furtherance of the above-mentioned good designs.

Local charity sermons were common. Westminster Free School, for example, received as much as £254 in 1814 and as little as £59 in 1821 from this source, though here as elsewhere there was reluctance to arrange charity sermons too often for fear that they would lose their effect.[13]

Difficulty was encountered in finding a site for the school buildings, because, it was explained in May 1824, local land-

owners were opposed to the idea of the use of land for such a
purpose:

> The Revd Dr D'Oyly explained to the meeting the cause of
> the delay . . . Enquiries had been made respecting several
> pieces of ground in the district, but the applications have
> been unsuccessful, as it has been found to be a general
> feeling among the owners of ground to be used for building,
> that by the erection of a *school* the property of the adjacent
> neighbourhood would be deteriorated in value.

(It was with some gratification three years later that the
treasurer was able to report that some of the objectors had
now become subscribers, and that the initial prejudice had
been overcome.) A site had eventually been chosen 'in the
Kennington Oval near the new road leading to Vauxhall', and
agreement had been reached to purchase the remainder of a
lease, which would ultimately revert to the Duchy of Cornwall.
Since 1337 the Manors of Kennington and Vauxhall had been
held by the Black Prince, Earl of Chester and Duke of Cornwall,
and his heirs, and these estates were at the beginning of the
nineteenth century (and still are today) administered by the
Duchy of Cornwall.[14] In 1834, on the reversion of the lease,
the committee did, in fact, agree with the Duchy on the purchase
of a new lease for the term of 'the life of Princess Victoria'. In
July 1824 tenders were accepted for the building of the schools
and houses for the two teachers, involving an estimated cost
of £1,315. In the event the land proved extremely difficult,
being subject to flooding from Vauxhall Creek. It had to be
raised and enclosed before building could begin, and, as Richard
Cannon pointed out: 'some expence has been unavoidably
incurred in draining and putting into a proper state, a part
of the public road round the Kennington Oval, which, until
now, has been scarcely passable, particularly in winter, or after
continued wet weather'. The architect was J. Bailey, of Buxton
Place, Lambeth, and the design has been described as 'a Regency
Greek building of modest size'.[15]

The financial difficulties of the school in future years were
frequently related to the debts incurred in the building of the
school, as a result of unexpectedly high expenses of this kind.
In January 1827, for example, Cannon referred to the unavoidably heavy building costs which resulted from:

the nature of the situation in which the buildings have been erected; a perfect swamp of itself; – subject also to inundations from the adjoining creek and from high tides; – without any means of drainage; with a bad road and footpath; – and in winter oftentimes inaccessible on account of the waters. But no other site of ground could at that time be obtained.

The space between the two school rooms was used for the construction of houses for the master and mistress of the two schools, who were appointed in late 1824 and early 1825. The first master in charge of the boys' school was Isaac Hitchen, who was one of a number of 'young men' recommended by the National Society, and who only accepted the post after first accepting one in Leeds (at £120 per annum) in October and returning to London for unexplained reasons a week or so later. Mr Hitchen was duly appointed on 4 November at a salary of £80 per year, plus £25 per year until his residence had been completed. In February of the following year a sub-committee selected two candidates from a number of applicants for the post of mistress of the girls' school, the committee itself interviewed these two, and appointed Rebecca Marchant at a salary of £50 per year, plus £18 per year until the house was finished. For the period from 1 November 1824 to 24 December 1825 the account book shows the master's salary and lodging allowance to have been £143.3s.10d., and that of the mistress £55.13s.4d. In 1826 the master and mistress both received a 'salary and gratuity', the former of £90 and the latter of £55.5s.0d. The following year the master received £95 and the mistress the same as the previous year. The importance of the school, in terms of size and status, can be judged from Hitchen's salary. Two years earlier a charity school in Tooting, some five miles away, had advertised for a new master:[16]

Wanted for the Charity School of Tooting a master, properly qualified to instruct about forty boys. Salary £40. per annum with a house free of charge.

The Kennington sponsors seem to have accepted as a matter of course that girls should be educated in equal numbers with boys, though it is clear that this was not accepted everywhere so easily. Burgess points out that it was only several years after its foundation that the National Society began to show concern about the extent of the provision being made for girls. The committee of the Society then began to draw attention to the inadequacy where it was evident. In 1818, for example, they answered an application for help from Llandudno with the suggestion 'that it would be extremely desirable to admit a larger number of girls than is at present indicated'. In 1821 they criticised an application from Park Royal School, Chelsea, on the grounds of 'the small provision made for the education of girls in the parish'.[17]

When informing the committee that it was nominating Mr Hitchen as 'Master for the Boys National School now forming in the Kennington district', the National Society took the opportunity to remind its members that 'before schools can be supplied with instructors from the Society it is usual for them to be united to the parent institution'. The Society, therefore, at the same time sent a copy of the 'plan of union'. Since the Kennington committee was not asking the Society for financial assistance (and did not do so at any future time, though on two occasions in 1825 and 1827 it almost did so), it did not have to comply with the general financial and other conditions of the Society. Schools had to be 'in union', however, before assistance of *any* kind was given, including the recommendation of teachers trained centrally by the Society at its School in Baldwin's Gardens. The committee decided that the schools 'be conducted according to the plan and principles of the National Society, and that a request for their being united to the National Society be immediately forwarded to Dr. Walmsley as Secretary to the said Society'. The children were to be instructed, the decision recorded, 'in the Liturgy and Catechism of the Established Church, and constantly to attend divine service in their parish Church, or other place of worship under the Establishment'. The committee accepted one of the regulations of the National Society in agreeing that 'no religious tracts shall be used in the school, but such as are contained in the catalogue of the Society for Promoting Christian Knowledge'. The committee's decision embodied the form of words published by the National Society itself in 1811, with regard to the use of the liturgy and catechism of the Established Church, attendance at a place of worship under the Establishment, and the use of S.P.C.K. religious material.[18] Generally speaking schools in union with the National Society did operate on this basis, accepting only the children of parents who were willing to agree to the Church of England conditions. Some schools did, however, make explicit decisions not to exclude the children of Dissenters. In its annual report for 1818, for example, the Society published a report from East Grinstead:[19]

> the benefit of education in this school is not refused to any child, on account of its parents being dissenters from the Church of England, or of its non-attendance at church on the Lord's Day, provided the parents or friends of the child undertake for its attendance with them, on the Lord's Day at some place of public worship.

This was more commonly the case in country districts where there was no other school. At Kennington the assumption must be that the children of nonconformists were not admitted, and not until a period of national controversy about this issue in the 1860s was a contrary view heard (in November 1865 the question arose on the committee 'as to the admission or rejection of the children of any denomination . . . and was resolved in the affirmative so that the admission of all children will be the rule'). No provision was made, however, in the earlier period for attendance at any church other than St Mark's.

The committee's plans had been for an intake of 200 boys and 200 girls, and numbers soon moved towards these targets. After the two schools had opened, the committee received at its monthly meetings a report on attendance: the number of boys on the roll had reached 185 in June 1825, at which time the girls' school had 110. In November the figures were 190 and 139 respectively, and in March of the following year 200 and 143.

The schools clearly established themselves quickly and effectively, carrying out the intentions of the founders:

> To accustom betimes the infant poor to good and orderly habits, – to instil into their minds an early knowledge of their civil and religious duties, – to guard them, as far as possible, from the seductions of vice, – and to afford them the means of becoming good Christians, as well as useful and industrious members of society.

Almost all public statements connected with the schools express their purpose in language similar to this, language to be found throughout the educational literature of the early nineteenth century. The committee at Kennington was conscious not only of its local but also its national mission: in describing the benefits of a Christian education it emphasised that 'the fullest experience has now established the fact, that Nations are more or less conspicuous for their morality and good conduct, in proportion as these blessings have been diffused among them'.

A set of 'orders, directions, and admonitions' to be observed by the children and their parents was issued by the committee, a document which gives the clearest picture of the way the committee intended the purposes of the school to be carried out. Children were to be from families within the parish 'who cannot afford to pay for their education', and were to be not less than six years old. School hours were to be 9–12 a.m. and 2–5 p.m. (2–4 p.m. from Michaelmas to Lady-day), six days a week, with Wednesday and Saturday afternoons free. (There is no evidence as to when Saturday schooling was discontinued, but it was probably well before the log books were begun in 1863.) Children were to gather at the school at 10 a.m. and 6 p.m. on Sundays in order to go as a body to church. Children were expected to be diligent and attentive:

> remembering, that they are sent to learn what is good and useful to themselves; and that they are educated in the knowledge and practice of the Christian religion, as professed and taught in the Church of England, with the hope of making them good Christians, and useful members of the community.

Children were to be sent to school 'in a clean and decent manner, with their hair cut short and combed, their face and hands washed, and their clothes well mended'. The ones who were best behaved and attended most regularly would be provided with Sunday clothes, which were 'to be put in a bag, provided for that purpose, and brought to the school every Monday morning, where they are to be kept until the following Saturday'. Offenders could be suspended or expelled, and parents were asked to 'forbear coming to the School' when their children were to be chastised.

It is clear from this and an accompanying document that the

committee were intending to influence the behaviour of the parents as much as that of the children. Parents were asked to co-operate with the committee on three points:

> *First*, By observing, as far as regards themselves, and by enforcing upon their children, the regulations of the school, without which little good can be effected; –
> *Secondly*, – By assisting their children in daily prayer, – by reading the Scriptures with them frequently, especially on the Sabbath-day, – and by their own regular attendance at the House of God; –
> *Thirdly*, – By the powerful efficacy of their own sober conversation and example.
> Remembering always what an awful responsibility they will incur in the sight of God, if, by their misconduct or neglect, they should counteract the good instruction given to their children, and divert them from the paths of innocence and happiness into those of vice and misery.

The parents, it was expected, would be aware of the paramount importance of the work of education being carried on by the committee. The regulations stipulated that when parents intended to take a child away from the school 'it is expected of them to inform the master or mistress thereof, or to attend the committee, and to state their reasons for removing the children'. In 1828 the committee reminded the teachers, with a different emphasis, 'that, in all cases of children quitting the schools, they expect . . . that the parent and child shall attend at the committee, to express thanks for the benefits received, – or to explain the cause of the child's removal'. The minutes of a committee meeting in July 1826 record that three parents 'had attended at the school and had expressed themselves grateful for the advantages their children had received from the school'.

One of the interesting features of the Kennington rules is the extent of their detail. National schools were generally covered in some way by a set of rules or regulations: the Devonshire committee, for example, issued a set of 'standing rules and regulations' for all its schools in the county, and the full list enables a useful comparison with Kennington to be made:[20]

RULES FOR THE GUIDANCE OF PARENTS

1. – They must send their children regularly to school at the proper hours, clean, washed, and combed, viz. nine in the morning, and two in the afternoon.
2. – That on Sundays they are to send their children to the school-room at such hours as shall be directed by the master, before they proceed to church.
3. – They must never detain them from school except from sickness, or by leave of the visitors. In the former case they must inform the master of the circumstance.
4. – No parents are permitted to take their children out of the school without their appearing before the committee.
5. – The parent or relative must be regular in the payment of one shilling per quarter, to be paid on every first Monday in January, April, July, and October.
6. – They must direct their children to pay strict attention to the following rules:

RULES FOR THE CHILDREN

1. – They must go directly to and from the school in an orderly manner.
2. – They must behave respectfully to their teachers, and strictly obey the directions given them.
3. – They must take the greatest care of their books and slates.
4. – They must be diligent whilst at school, and behave with the greatest reverence during prayers, or divine service at church.
5. – They must be kind one to another, and never tell a lie, cheat, steal, or swear.

The managers of the Kennington schools, in their dealings with pupils and parents, clearly had well-defined purposes in mind, and they were well content with the early social and educational success. A report published in 1827 emphasised that the committee believed that

the peculiar benefits of this institution have fully answered the warmest expectations of its friends: – that the instruction they have been able to bestow has been eagerly sought,

highly appreciated, and gratefully accepted by the poor; –
that the children, who have passed through the school, have
been greatly benefitted and improved, and well fitted for
the various situations they have to occupy.

Notes

A bound volume of minutes and various other documents, printed and
manuscript, 1823–40.

A bound volume of receipts and accounts and other documents, 1824–46.

MS 'amount of collections at St. Mark's Church – Kennington, for the
District Charity Schools'.

1 Rollo Laird Clowes, 'History of
   the Manor of Kennington in the
   County of Surrey', I, p. 1.
2 Thomas Allen, *The History and
   Antiquities of the Parish of
   Lambeth*, p. 9.
3 H. H. Montgomery, *The History of
   Kennington and its Neighbourhood*,
   pp. 137–9; Allen, *History and
   Antiquities*, pp. 381–2.
4 *Ibid.*, p. 440; Survey of London,
   XXVI, *The Parish of St. Mary
   Lambeth*, pt II, p. 1; *The Victoria
   History of the County of Surrey*, IV
   (1967 edn), p. 447; Adna Ferrin
   Weber, *The Growth of Cities in the
   Nineteenth Century* (1963 edn),
   p. 46.
5 Clowes, 'History of the Manor', I,
   p. 4.
6 G. E. Eades, *Historic London*,
   p. 207.
7 Clowes, 'History of the Manor', I,
   p. 31; Allen, *History and
   Antiquities*, pp. 382, 440.
8 House of Commons resolution,
   quoted in Montgomery, *History
   of Kennington*, p. 129.
9 Survey of London, XXIII, *South
   Bank and Vauxhall*, pt I, general
   editor Sir Howard Roberts, p. 123;
   Allen, *History and Antiquities*,
   p. 344
10 Lambeth Census, 1851, Kennington 1st pt, H.O. 107 1573 2 1, p. 2
11 Later Bishop of Chichester, where
   there is a college of education
   named after him.
12 Reproduced from the *Stamford
   Mercury* in Rex C. Russell, *A
   History of Schools and Education
   in Lindsey, Lincolnshire 1800–
   1902*, pt three, pp. 103–4.
13 H. J. Burgess, 'The Educational
   History of the National Society
   1811–1833', p. 223.
14 Survey of London, XXVI, p. 2.
15 *Ibid.*, p. 15.
16 Quoted in Pamela C. Lewis, 'The
   Early Charity Schools and
   National Schools of Tooting and
   Streatham'.
17 Burgess, 'Educational History of
   the National Society', p. 56.
18 H. J. Burgess, *Enterprise in
   Education*, p. 29.
19 *Seventh Annual Report of the
   National Society* (London, 1818),
   Appendix II.
20 'Standing Rules and Regulations
   formed by the Society for
   promoting the Education of the
   Poor, in the County of Devon and
   City of Exeter, in the Principles
   of the Established Church, and
   according to Dr. Bell's Plan',
   reproduced in *First Annual Report
   of the National Society*, p. 36.

Chapter three

Schooling 1824-40

The monitorial system

Although, as we have seen, the schools were conducted 'according to the plan and principles of the National Society', the committee's records contain little about the curriculum and the day-to-day working of the system; it was normal, however, for National schools to carry out Dr Bell's Madras system down to the smallest detail. Although the two Kennington Schools considered separately were not excessively large by urban monitorial school standards, only that system would have permitted up to 200 children to be taught by a single master or mistress (National schools elsewhere had 500 children or more under a single master).

Dr Bell's system was described as possessing 'a simplicity and certainty in its operations, that give scope to the exertions of the quickest mind, while they supply energy and activity to the dullest'.[1] The system was based on repetition of simple lessons under the guidance of the monitors (often called 'teachers' or 'assistants' in National schools), and a process of promotions and demotions which gave the scope to the quickest and the energy to the dullest. As a general rule under the National system, the central area of the single large school room was used by groups or 'classes' of children standing in squares for instruction by their monitors, and the outer area was occupied by desks, facing outwards to the wall, for writing purposes.

The system was cheaper to operate than schools which required more adult teachers, and under the Madras system 'a large school will, in a few months, supply an almost indefinite number of masters; to whom at their entrance on the stage of life, the most moderate salary will be an object', until they grow old enough to look for 'more lucrative employment, leave and make way for 'a succession of other teachers equally prepared'.[2] The National and British Societies both trained masters and mistresses to operate this simple piece of machinery (the British system was in practice little different from the National one, but its religious content was undenominational). The monitors were normally rewarded for their services, under the system of rewards which – together with a parallel system of punishments – dominated monitorial schools. The first reference to the payment of monitors at Kennington is probably in 1829–30, when a reference to £3.9s.8d. in the expenditure as 'rewards for children' no doubt includes the payment of monitors. After the school had introduced the payment of weekly 'school pence' by the children in 1835 the system was regularised, and the monitors and their assistants (here referred to as 'teachers') were to receive payments as laid down by the committee:

> that out of the sums paid by the children the following allowances be given to the monitors and teachers of the several classes in each school; viz.

To the 2 monitors	6d. pr. week each:
To the 2 teachers of the first classes	3d. pr. week each:
To the teachers of the other classes	2d. pr. week each.

What this meant in practice can be seen from the table of payments made for the quarter ending in April 1836 (Table 2):

Later in this chapter we shall see more of the rewards and punishments at Kennington; although it may have operated there with less complexity than at many other National schools,

Table 2

Boys	s.	d.	Girls	s.	d.
1 First class teacher	5.	6.	1 First class teacher	3.	6.
4 Teachers	4.	6.	5 Teachers	7.	6.
6 Assistants	5.	8.	4 Assistants	4.	6.
	15.	8.		15.	6.

The number of children on the books of the school at this time was 184 boys and 152 girls.

the monitorial system depended heavily on a pattern of incentives. The Devonshire schools, for example, adopted the popular 'tickets of merit' system:[3]

> The master of the school shall be entrusted with tickets of merit, which he is to distribute as he thinks proper. The value of the tickets to be as under-mentioned, half of which value to be paid by the visitors every Friday afternoon, and the remaining half to be entered by them in a book, called the fund book, and the children are to receive the amount of the sums opposite their names on their discharge from the school . . . In case the children leave the school improperly, the same to be forfeited.

Value

The usher for 6 tickets,	12d.	to receive 6d.	Fund book 6d.
Sub-usher	8d.	4d.	4d.
Monitor of the day	10d.	5d.	5d.
Teachers each	6d.	3d.	3d.
Assistant teachers	2d.	1d.	1d.

Besides which rewards, every boy who shall be found by the register to have been at the head of his class twice in the course of the week, to receive a ticket, six of which will be valued one penny, to be paid him immediately.

A charity school established in 1813 at Streatham, some four miles south of the Oval, was associated with, but not in union with, the National Society; it adopted many of the practices of the Baldwin's Gardens school, including occasional cash rewards (for example, three shillings in 1815 to a boy who 'was very useful in the school'), and the distribution of medals, prayer books and clothing. The trustees of this school decided in 1813 that 'medals be given to each of the boys as may be found to deserve them', and white and silver medals are mentioned in their minutes in 1815 and 1825.[4]

The reason why little information was recorded about the operation of the monitorial system itself at Kennington was that the system was so well known, and so universally accepted as the cheapest and most desirable form of school organisation for the children of the poor, that it seemed to require no description or comment. In 1827 the committee explicitly commented that 'they will not occupy the time of the subscribers with arguments in support of that general plan of national education, to the utility and excellence of which the voice of experience has, from so many quarters, borne the clearest and amplest testimony'.

Attendance

Ensuring regular attendance by the children and keeping them at school long enough to acquire even a basic literacy were two of the most persistent problems faced by nineteenth-century schools. Surveys by statistical and other organisations in the 1830s showed how serious these problems were in manufacturing and commercial towns like Manchester and Liverpool, and also in London. The returns of early parliamentary committees, such as that of Henry Brougham on the education of children of the poor in the metropolis in the late 1810s, and Lord Kerry's parliamentary enquiry of 1833, also showed the extent of these problems as well as those of the inadequate supply of schools. One of Lord Kerry's illustrations of the problem of the turnover of children in the schools was a National school where the books were apparently well kept; it had admitted nearly 900 children in a period of eleven months, but there were never more than 400 on the books at any one time.[5] The census of education conducted in 1851 estimated (optimistically) that the school life of a working-class child was about four years between the ages of five and fifteen, but, in the words of a later comment, 'as the attendance was very irregular, it is doubtful whether the actual school life (reckoned by the attendance, not by the time during which their names were on the school registers) can be fairly estimated at more than half that period'.[6]

After the creation by the government of the Committee of the Privy Council on Education in 1839, and the appointment of the first of H.M. Inspectors of schools, the extent and reality of the problems became more clear. In every kind of area the inspectors showed how poor and irregular attendance could be, and how short was the total length of school life. The inspectors' early reports are full of examples such as these from the same page of a report on schools in rural Cambridgeshire in 1845:[7]

Swaffham Bulbeck, 11th March. – 98 boys and girls. Attendance varies according to season, from 53 to 100. Age from $4\frac{1}{2}$ to 14 . . .

Swavesey, 24th February. – Girls, 40 present. Boys 52. The attendance irregular; of 75 girls on the books, about 20 attend in September and 40 in December. Of 86 boys, 50 is the average attendance. In both schools the ages vary from 3 to 4 to 14 years.

A National school in urban Stockport, to take the most dramatic example in a report for 1840, had an average attendance of 100 during a six-month period when 660 names had appeared on the books. Whereas many of the schools in Lancashire showed more reasonable or improving attendance figures at this time, attendance at this particular school was described as 'latterly on decrease, through cold weather'.[8] Schools such as this were also open to serious fluctuations when depression in trade reduced the number of factory children in attendance on the half-time system which operated after the Factory Act of 1833. In the year preceding the opening of the Kennington Schools the Church of England organisation sponsoring schools in Durham conducted a detailed enquiry into attendance at three schools (Barrington, Durham and Sunderland). It found that in the three schools:

> upon an average 1 child in 3, 1 in 7, and 1 in 10, (or nearly 1–6th of the whole) have been daily, from various causes, with and without leave, from school. It is clear, then, that the benefits of good instruction must have been not only administered with confusion and inefficiency, but totally thrown away to such proportions of the numbers who should have enjoyed them: and as different boys would be absent at different periods, the general character of the school . . . will suffer in the same degree.

Overall numbers had declined during the year, because 'the demand for children in manufactories, and in other occupations, particularly in Gateshead, is very much increased'.[9]

At Kennington the number of children on the books remained more or less stable, generally approaching 200 boys and about 150 to 180 girls. After an examination of attendance figures in December 1827 the committee 'regretted to observe the numbers of absentees on some days', though they realised the difficulty 'particularly at this season of the year, of enforcing the due attendance of the children, many of whom are very young; –

D

many are very poor – barely clothed, and almost without shoes'. A report to the general meeting the following year mentioned that 'the recent winter which has been unusually wet, has occasioned a decrease of the numbers, particularly of the younger children'. The introduction of the fee of a penny a week in 1835 appears not to have affected numbers; if anything, reported the treasurer, in the week following the introduction of payments, numbers had increased. In the winter of 1839 attendance was still being 'much affected by the continuously wet and unfavourable weather'. Two months later, at the end of January 1840, it was reported to the committee that forty-two children still on the school books had not attended since Christmas; it was decided to remove them from the strength of the school, and they would be classified as re-admissions if they re-appeared in person. Not until the log books are studied for the period after 1862 does the range of reasons for absence become more apparent.

In the early 1830s the committee began to receive regular information not only about the number of children on the school books, admissions and withdrawals, but also average attendance. In May 1833, for example, 'the committee had occasion to remark on the great proportion of absentees in the boys schools; the average number present being *142 only* out of *206*, leaving 64 absent'. In November the same year the number of boys on the books was 197 with an average attendance of 139, and the number of girls 173 with an average attendance of 130 (see Table 3).

Table 3

Date	Boys		Girls	
	No. in school	Average attendance	No. in school	Average attendance
30th May 1833	206	142 (69%)	170	not given
28th November 1833	197	139 (71%)	173	130 (75%)
26th May 1836	181	154 (85%)	153	132 (86%)
28th May 1840	172	157 (91%)	153	132 (86%)
26th November 1840	184	160 (87%)	162	141 (87%)

In January 1837 the minutes do not even bother to record the average attendance figures, and merely comment that 'the continuance of wet and cold weather, and the prevalence of much sickness, have been the causes of a very thin attendance of the children at school and at church for several weeks past'. There seems to have been an improvement in attendance during the 1830s, however, and it is likely that these figures were better than for most similar schools.

The committee, it should be added, took the problem of irregular attendance very seriously – though humanely. As a result of the absences in the winter of 1827 they authorised the master and mistress to collect from 'such children as are disposed to contribute, the sum of one penny per week', and the contributions would be supplemented by the committee for the purpose of buying shoes for the children. In the winter of 1839, in recording the children's poor attendance, they added that 'every attention is paid to their comfort, as well as their instruction, by keeping the school rooms dry, and warm, and properly ventilated, in reference to the health of the children'. The committee took a serious view of truancy and persistent absence, however. In April 1825, only a few months after the school had opened, the master reported to the committee 'that Thomas and John Salmon, – Nicholas and Robert Chaplain, – and John Burton, have been absent for some time without leave. It was resolved, that the boys named be discontinued as belonging to the school.' In June 1826 the father of one boy, James Griffiths, was summoned to meet the committee 'in consequence of the repeated irregularity of the boy in his attendance'; in August, 'notwithstanding the admonition and reproof conveyed to the father of James Griffiths and the means adopted for correcting the irregularity of the boy', he had persisted in breaking the school rules (it is not clear whether this refers to behaviour other than irregular attendance), and was dismissed from the school. In January 1833 John Allen, 'who was reported to be an incorrigible truant player . . . was in consequence ordered to be expelled'. The interesting point about such cases is that they are explicitly emphasised in the committee's minutes as exceptions. In the latter case, for example, the minute underlines that 'the conduct of the children was reported to be good, and their attendance regular, considering the season of the year, with one exception . . .'.

It is clear from some of this discussion that at least a substantial number of the children were from extremely poor
families, yet the school was able to maintain a reasonable
attendance record. The committee reported, some two years
after the boys' school had opened, on 1 November 1824, that
since that date 368 boys had been admitted, of whom 127 had
since obtained employment, 39 had left the neighbourhood
with their parents, 2 had died and 200 were still at school.
The girls' school had opened on 2 March 1825, and since that
date 270 girls had been admitted, of whom 69 had 'found
employment in service', 51 had left the neighbourhood, 4 had
died, 3 had 'been discontinued' and 143 were still 'under the
course of instruction'.

For no apparent reason the treasurer, Richard Cannon, wrote
down his views in 1840 on the question of attendance since the
school had opened. Although the committee minutes comment
very little on attendance in the first decade or so of the schools'
life, it is clear that Cannon at least had harboured some bitter
views about the parents. The tone of this document is different
from anything existing for the earlier period, and as an important document to set alongside the statistics on attendance
at the schools it is worth giving in full:

> The average weekly attendance of the children, – both boys
> and girls, as shown by the weekly payment-books, is very
> satisfactory, particularly when it is considered, that for
> several years after these schools were established in 1825,
> and previous to the *payment system* being introduced in
> 1835, much difficulty was experienced in enforcing the
> proper attendance of the children; – the parents, in many
> instances, seemed to think that they were conferring a
> favor on the subscribers by sending their children to the
> schools; – many of the children, who attended, were
> oftentimes sent out to enquire and hunt after the *absentees*;
> – and false and mean excuses were, too frequently, made by
> the parents for the absence of their children, such as, pleas
> of sickness, – want of shoes, – &c. &c., thus teaching their
> children, in early life, in practising deceit, and in evading
> duty.
> The working of the schools upon the present system has
> happily counteracted, and greatly tended to reduce, these

evils: – the responsibility for the attendance of the children has, in a great degree, been thrown (where it ought to be) *upon the parents*, who are informed on the admission of their children, that they themselves must enforce their *attendance* as well as *cleanliness*, and that their proper instruction will of course depend on the joint efforts of the parents.

It is now but rarely necessary to send after *absentees*; – and still less rare to be obliged to have recourse to punishment for absence.

Compulsion and severity are now no longer necessary to enforce attendance, or the general rules of the schools.

The change of system has thus produced an improvement in the moral feeling of the parents as well as children.

Some of the comments, such as those about shoes and severity in the early years, are in a different tone from the committee's minutes on such topics, and it may be that the minutes were not a true reflection of the situation, or that Cannon was simply becoming older and more jaundiced. It is likely that, as the figures have shown, attendance was improving in the late 1830s and he felt obliged to express his indignation about the earlier years simply in order to point the contrast. It is interesting that the attitude of parents who thought they were 'conferring a favor on the subscribers' had altogether escaped mention in the committee's private papers and public announcements. It is obvious, however, that the school had not found it easy to enforce attendance before this date, and though the average attendance in the schools was rising, it cannot have been any less easy in October 1840!

Cannon's reference to the 'payment system' is to a decision taken by a meeting of the subscribers in November 1834, and implemented the following year. The subject had been raised at the July meeting and postponed, pending enquiries about the system of payments that had been introduced in some other schools. Cannon reported back to the November meeting, and also read 'extracts from the evidence given before a committee of the House of Commons in the last session of parliament on the subject of the *education of the poor*'. The meeting adopted the following resolution:

That this meeting is of opinion that the system of weekly payments should be adopted in these schools from and after

Easter next, and that a committee . . . be appointed to
confer in such manner as they may consider desirable with
the directors of the other National Schools in the parish,
with a view to making practice in this respect uniform.

A meeting with representatives from other National schools
in Lambeth was held in December, and produced at least one
strong letter of protest, signed by a 'friend to the Stockwell
National Schools'; this letter protested that the Brixton
deputation had no mandate to attend, and that 'the Kennington
Committee have *already resolved to adopt the pay system*'. The
notice of this meeting had indicated that 'the plan of requiring
a small weekly payment from the parents or friends of the
children, has been found in various National Schools to be
"most beneficial" '. How would it benefit 'a poor man, to
require him *to pay for the education* of his child, when he has
hitherto had the privilege of sending that child to the same
school, *free of expense?*' Was it not a breach of faith to convert
an institution founded (in 1815, in the case of the Stockwell
schools), to be ' "*open to the free and gratuitous* admission of all
who require admittance", into one accessible only by money
payments?' In other areas, where the schools were poor and
wealthy neighbours few, payments might be a question of need;
the letter quotes from a National Society report:

> The *National Society* in countenancing the occasional
> adoption of the *pay system*, have expressly guarded their
> recommendation, by desiring its application only to such
> schools as (to use their own strong language) were *struggling
> for existence*; – '*to prevent what they must deem a public
> calamity*' – '*the suspension or discontinuance of even a single
> National school*' (see report for 1827, pages 12 & 13).

The protest was without avail, at least as far as Kennington
was concerned, and a special meeting of the committee was
convened in April 1835 to decide on the steps to be taken to
carry out the November resolution. The committee decided
that parents should be informed:

1. That the parents of the children, attending these schools,
   shall in future pay one penny per week for each child on
   every Monday morning; – and that the payment of such
   sum shall commence on Monday the 27th April 1835.

2. That an account be kept by the master and mistress . . .
and that the amount be paid over to the gentlemen of the
committee.

The accounts for 1835 for the first time, therefore, record as
income the 'amount of weekly payments by the children for 32
weeks, at one penny each per week', the total being £37.13s.6d.
Totals for the next four years varied between £50 and £54,
somewhat less than the amount normally raised by one morning
and one evening sermon preached on behalf of the schools.
Donations to the school in 1835 were over £250 and annual
subscriptions in that year brought in nearly £200. The income
from school pence was therefore of minor importance – the main
purpose probably being to encourage a more committed attitude
among parents, and to remove any sense that the schools,
being free, were somehow similar to pauper out-relief (which
itself was under attack, particularly under the Poor Law
Amendment Act of the previous year).

The 1851 education census discussed the merits and demerits
of making parents pay for their children's education, and the
view expressed by its author was no doubt similar to that in
the minds of the subscribers when they took their decision. The
argument that a penny or two pence a week was beyond the
means of labouring men was not accepted in the census report:
the argument, it maintained, applied only to paupers in workhouses – and their children were in any case being educated
free. As for the rest: 'when it is considered that the working
classes annually spend upon intoxicating liquors nearly
£50,000,000 sterling, it can hardly be asserted generally that
the children are retained at home because the parents are
unable to advance 1d. or 2d. per week'. In many free schools,
the report indicated, 'attendance of scholars is less numerous
and much less constant than in schools which require a fee'.[10]
It was this kind of argument that had probably weighed with
Richard Cannon and the other Kennington subscribers. Cannon
was clearly of the opinion in 1840 that the introduction of school
pence had contributed to making attendance more 'numerous'
and 'constant'. In 1846 the committee referred to the children's
contributions 'by which regular attendance is insured'. It is
possible – though there is no direct evidence to this effect – that
one consequence of the introduction of payments was to alter

the social composition of the schools, by eliminating from the
books the poorest children and attracting children from some
better-off families. This would help to account for the improved
attendance. There is indeed direct evidence – as we shall see –
that the social composition was changing by the 1870s, and it
is just possible that the process began to a limited extent with
the introduction of school pence. There was in any case, as
A. E. Dobbs has pointed out, a tendency for voluntary education
movements (and the same would be true of housing and some
other movements) gradually to cater for a higher class of the
population than was originally intended. The main stimulus
to philanthropy, Dobbs indicates, had always been 'the hope
of dealing with the sources of crime and destitution and civilising
a class whose ignorance was a menace to society'. The difficulty,
especially in urban districts, was to reconcile this aim with
actual schemes of education:[11]

> The tone of a school and its standard of discipline would
> improve in proportion to its success. It would attract by
> degrees a superior class of children, and appeal to a more
> respectable and fastidious class of parents. The managers,
> finding it difficult to accommodate all under the same
> system of discipline and instruction, would drift from their
> original aim into safer paths of financial security.

This is a possible explanation of what was beginning to happen
at Kennington.

From 1832 the annual report began to record not only total
numbers, admissions and withdrawals, but also the distribution
of the children according to age. The information about this
was introduced in that and subsequent years by what was
obviously a carefully worded formula:

> The following statement of the ages of the children, in both
> schools, is given, in order that the subscribers may see,
> that no children of either sex are retained in the schools
> beyond a period at which they may be fit to perform, with
> advantage to their employers and to themselves, the duties
> of the ordinary stations of life for which they are destined.

It is likely that this was meant to allay the fears of middle-class
parents that the children in the 'charity schools' were getting
an education which would raise them above their 'stations of

life' and enable them to compete with the children of their betters. The age distribution of the children in 1832 was as shown in Table 4.

Table 4

	Boys	Girls
Above six and under eight years of age	90	50
Above eight and under ten	82	58
Above ten and under twelve	31	38
Above twelve and under thirteen	4	14
Above thirteen	2	3
Total now in the schools	209	163

A year later the number of boys and girls between the ages of twelve and thirteen were six and seven respectively, and above thirteen there were no boys and two girls. Another year later there were sixteen boys and eight girls between twelve and thirteen, and three boys and four girls above the age of thirteen. Not until 1880, it should be remembered, was a school-leaving age of thirteen established by law, and then only in theory, as exemptions were easy to gain from the age of ten. In the years 1832–4, the proportion of children on the school books over the age of ten rose from just under to well over a quarter.

In fixing a lower age limit of six the Kennington schools had fallen into line with a common practice, since two or three to six had become a widely accepted age range for infant schools from the early 1820s, and infant schools had come to be seen after Robert Owen's model had been adopted, as preparatory to the work of the monitorial schools.[12] By the end of the 1830s it is known that two Church infant schools were functioning in the parish – one in North Brixton, with 180 children, and the other in White Hart Street, Kennington, with some 130 children. In 1839 an appeal on behalf of the White Hart Street infant school, which had 'very recently been established', and the Kennington Schools was made jointly to the Duchy of Cornwall. It is unlikely that infant schools connected with the Church or the National Society could have existed in the vicinity at an earlier date without their being mentioned in the Kennington records. The decision to make six the entry age was therefore in accordance more with National Society principles than local need. In some parts of the country six was, indeed, a late age of entry even for National schools in the 1840s.

From the period up to 1840 there are few clues as to the schools' official holiday arrangements, and even those relate only to the summer. In June 1828 the committee agreed that 'holidays for three weeks should be allowed to commence on Monday the 20th June' (this is the only time within this period that the committee recorded any such decision, although holidays were obviously fixed by the committee year by year on an *ad hoc* basis). The second reference occurs in the report of a committee meeting on 27 August 1829, on which date no report was presented about the boys' school, it 'being closed on account of holidays, and the master absent on account of sickness'. The girls' school, on the other hand, had been re-opened after a fortnight's vacation. Whether two or three weeks' holiday was normal in the summer is therefore not clear; nor is it clear when the holiday was normally taken. By 1845 annual holidays are known to have totalled four weeks (income from payments by the children that year were for forty-eight weeks). It is probable that two or three weeks in the summer, a week at Christmas, a few days at Easter and one day at Whitsuntide was the pattern of holidays in this period.

Curriculum

The committee's minutes, published reports and other records are almost silent on the content of the curriculum for the first ten years or so of the school's existence – probably, as we have seen, because it was taken for granted. A public statement in 1825 talked about the 'progress of all the children in useful knowledge, and that of the girls in industrious work'. The latter phrase is frequently explained in early reports and notices of sermons on behalf of the schools: the 1827 report, for example, which covered the period since the schools had opened, discusses the girls' needlework:

> In the girls' school the afternoons of four days in each week
> are devoted to needle work: regular prices have been fixed
> for the several kinds of work, and a general account is kept

of the whole. The amount of the sums earned by these
means to the end of the year 1826, was £28.7s.1d. This sum,
after defraying the expense of articles necessary for carrying
on the work, has been expended in providing a portion of
the deserving girls with cloaks, bonnets, frocks, and tippets,
in which they appear at Church on Sundays.

The report the following year explained that 'a supply of needlework having been obtained from families in the neighbourhood,
the girls have continued to be employed in that work on the
afternoons of four days in each week' (the sum earned that year
was £15.8s.3d.). A list of 'regular prices' was published at
various times, including, for example, the following, in 1837:

*The following list of prices for needle-work at the Kennington
Girls' School is inserted for the information of families who
may be disposed to encourage the works of industry in the
female branch of this institution.*

		s.	d.	s.	d.
A fine shirt, trimmed	from	2	6 to 3	0
A plain shirt				2	0
A fine shift, trimmed				2	0
A plain shift				1	6
A night shift, trimmed	from	2	0 to 2	6
Collars		0	4 to 0	6
Sheets, per pair		0	10 to 1	0
Pillow-cases, per pair		0	4 to 0	6
Table-cloths		0	4 to 1	0
Cambric handkerchiefs, per dozen				2	0
Common ditto				1	2
Marking, per dozen				0	3
Towels, dusters, &c. per dozen		0	4 to 1	0

*The work is done with great care, and to be paid for on
delivery.*

This emphasis in the girls' school work is reminiscent of the
eighteenth-century charity school, and particularly the school
of industry.

The teaching of reading, writing and arithmetic are only
occasionally mentioned, but moral and religious training is
inferred or explicit in everything relating to the school. These

formed the main content of the National system of education
generally, and it is unlikely that Kennington was different in
any important respect. That these formed at least the major
part of the curriculum can be seen from an important paragraph
in the annual report drafted for the subscribers in 1840:

> The mode of instruction continues to be carried on according
> to the approved system. The alternate lessons in reading, –
> writing, – arithmetic, – scriptural exercises, including cate-
> chismal questions, &c, continue to be practised according
> to a table, which prescribes the lessons for each hour. The
> *dictation-lesson* which is now directed by the London
> Diocesan Board of Education to be practised in the National
> Schools generally, as combining the means of instruction in
> writing and orthography, has been practised in the Ken-
> nington District Schools ever since their first establishment
> and has always been found to produce the best effects in
> the improvement of the children.

The 'approved system' of both the National and the British
Societies consisted, as we have seen, of the transmission of
some very basic skills. No time-table of the Kennington Schools
in this period has survived, but it is not difficult to picture the
kind of day that the children will have spent from information
relating to other schools. In 1814, for example, the National
Society published the daily 'employment' of the children at
Baldwin's Gardens:[13]

MORNING

> The schools open precisely at nine with prayers, consisting
> of the 2d and 3rd collects of morning service, the Lord's
> Prayer, and 'the Grace of our Lord', read by one of the
> children; and every child not present at prayers, and not
> assigning a satisfactory reason for absence, is detained after
> school-hours from five to thirty minutes.
>   After prayers the first aisle cipher till ten – learn by
> heart religious exercises till half-past ten – write till
> eleven – and read till the schools are dismissed, at twelve.
>   Second aisle write till half-past nine – learn religious
> exercises till ten – read till eleven – and cipher till twelve.
>   Third aisle learn religious exercises till half-past nine – and
> read and write alternately till twelve.

AFTERNOON

The schools re-open at two. The girls' school, still in classes with teachers, assistants, &c. learn knitting and needle-work till half-past four, and arithmetical tables till five.

The boys' school – first aisle cipher till three – write till half-past three – read till half-past four, – learn arithmetical tables till five.

Second aisle write till half-past two – read till half-past three – cipher till half-past four, – and learn arithmetical tables till five.

Third aisle read and write till half-past four, and learn arithmetical tables or cipher till five; at which hour both schools are dismissed with the Gloria Patria, sung by the children after prayers read by one of the children.

Thirty years later the boys' time-table at Baldwin's Gardens was as shown in Table 5.[14]

A parallel 'employment' (in this case called an 'order of occupation') for boys at British Society schools can be judged from the following document issued for guidance by the Society in 1815. This is the model recommended for Mondays:

Assemble – 9 o/clock.
> The boys as they enter take their seats in their respective writing classes, and commence writing from dictation; at the same time the reading monitors are exercised in reading at their draft stations.

15m. p. 9. The school door is closed – the master reads aloud a chapter from the Holy Scriptures; after which the whole school commences the arithmetical tables from dictation: in the meantime each monitor takes an account of the absentees . . . at the same time he collects from each boy his text paper (a slip of paper on which boys wrote the text of a sermon heard the day before).

30m. p. 9. The boys are drafted into semicircles for reading; at which they are exercised (by monitors) till

30m. p. 10. When they return to their writing classes.

30m. p. 11. The good and bad boys are called out from their seats, and are rewarded or punished accordingly; at the same time the whole school commences writing

Table 5

TIME TABLE

at the National Society's Central Boys' School, December, 1845

A.M.

$9\frac{1}{4}$ to $9\frac{3}{4}$ $10\frac{1}{2}$ 11 $11\frac{1}{2}$ 12–

Doors shut at Nine o'Clock. Prayers & Singing the whole School

Class					
1	Catechism and Liturgy, with Scripture Proofs	Ciphering Revisal	Writing upon Paper	Reading and Exposition of the Holy Bible	
2	Catechism and Liturgy with Scripture Proofs	Writing upon Paper	Ciphering Old Rules	Reading with Explanation and Grammar	
3	Catechism with Proofs	Arithmetic Old Rules	Reading New Testament	Linear Drawing	Mental Calculations and Arithmetical Tables
4	Catechism with Proofs	Reading New Testament	Linear Drawing	Arithmetic Revisal of Old Rules	Outlines of Geography and Arithmetic Tables alternately
5	Catechism with Analysis and Scripture Proofs	Writing from Dictation or Memory	Reading New Testament	Ciphering Old Rules	Arithmetic Tables & Spelling on alternate days
6	Catechism with Analysis	Ciphering Revisal	Reading and Spelling	Writing upon Paper	Writing upon Slates; Tables Definitions &c
7	Catechism with Analysis	Reading and Spelling	Writing in Desks	Arithmetic &c	Arithmetical Tables
8	Catechism with Analysis	Linear Drawing	Arithmetic Numeration	Reading & Spelling from Miscellaneous Books	
9	Catechism	Arithmetic Numeration	Reading	Writing in Desks from Black Board	Spelling in Classes
10	Catechism	Reading	Writing in Desks from Black Board	Spelling and Reading	Addition and Multiplication Tables
11	Catechism	Reading	Addition and Multiplication Tables	Spelling and Reading	Writing in Desks from Black Board

Theory and practice of Vocal Music on Tuesday and Friday Mornings

P.M.

2 to 2½	3	3½	4¼	4¾
Drawing on Mons. Weds. & Fridays Mental Arithmetic Tuesdays & Thursdays	Reading History of England and Hogarth's Geography alternately, with Etymology and Grammar		Ciphering New Rules	Geography and Elements of Astronomy
New Testament	Linear Drawing	Arithmetical Tables	Ciphering New Rules	Writing from Dictation, and Geography on alternate days
Writing upon Paper	Reading Miscellaneous Books with Explanation & Grammar		Dictation and Geography on alternate days	Ciphering New Rules
Ciphering New Rules	Writing upon Paper	Reading, Explanation, Spelling and Grammar		Writing from Dictation Terms in Geography &c
Linear Drawing	Ciphering New Rules	Writing upon Paper	Reading Miscellaneous Books Explanation, Spelling and Grammar	
Reading New Testament	Linear Drawing	Arithmetic New Rules	Reading and Spelling	Definitions in Geography and Grammar
Religious Instruction	Reading and Spelling	Arithmetic from Black Board	Linear Drawing	Definitions in Geography and Grammar
Arithmetic from Black Board	Definitions in Geography and Grammar	Writing in Desk from Black Board	Reading and Religious Instruction	Arithmetic Tables
Arithmetic from Black Board	Religious Instruction	Tuesdays & Thursdays Drawing; Mondays Wednesdays & Fridays Writing on Slates	Reading and Spelling	Arithmetic Tables
Arithmetic from Black Board	Religious Instruction	Reading and Spelling	Writing on Slates	Arithmetic Tables
Religious Instruction	Addition and Subtraction from Black Board	Writing on Slates in Seats	Addition and Multiplication Tables	Arithmetic Tables

Books, Slates &c collected – Prayers & Singing the whole School the arithmetical tables from dictation.

45m. p. 11. The monitors are ranged in front of the plat-
form, and read aloud the Ten Commandments and the
rules of the school.

12 o/clock. The school is dismissed.

AFTERNOON

Assemble – 2 o/clock.

The boys as they enter take their seats in their
respective writing classes and commence writing from
dictation; at the same time the reading monitors are
exercised in reading at their draft stations.

15m. p. 2. The school door is closed; after which the whole
school commences writing the arithmetical tables from
dictation: in the meantime each monitor takes an
account of the absentees . . .

30m. p. 2. The boys are drafted into semicircles for reading;
at which they are exercised until

30m. p. 3. When they return to their writing classes. The
eighth class now write on paper.

30m. p. 4. The good and bad boys are called out from their
seats and are rewarded or punished accordingly; at the
same time the whole school commences writing the
arithmetical tables from dictation, as in the morning.

45m. p. 4. The master reads aloud a chapter from the Holy
Scriptures.

5 o/clock. The school is dismissed.[15]

Repetition and 'exercise' were obviously the basis of this
system – the monitor taking his 'class' through, for example,
the spelling of words by the constant repetition of syllables
or the writing down of figures from dictation and the working
of simple sums. At the beginning the younger children wrote
in sand, but slates were universally adopted, and writing on
paper was in this period a luxury for the senior classes. By
1840 monitorial schools had begun very often to introduce
other subjects – mainly geography – and to vary the methods
used slightly, but the quality of the monitors placed strict
limitations on what could be attempted.

An example from an inspector's report on a school in Norwich
in 1840 summarises the position at that date. This was a model

school selected for the training of future National school masters and mistresses for the diocese, the average age of the 114 boys present at the inspector's visit was about ten and the monitors were between ten and fourteen years of age. Teaching was almost entirely on the monitorial method. Books included S.P.C.K. texts, a grammar, a class singing book, Bible and Testament, an arithmetic book and some geography books. There were maps, natural history and geography prints, a table of the relative heights of mountains, a cabinet of objects to illustrate lessons, an arithmetic frame, diagrams and two blackboards. Even this attempt to provide a central training system for monitors in the area was able to produce only limited results:[16]

> the scope and intention of the elementary processes of teaching have been enlarged, and it is to be hoped may gradually bring forth their fruit; but I am unable to say that at present they have resulted in much actual acquire-ment. The monitors, four of whom had acted two years, and three one year in that capacity, were unable to read with accuracy, or to show that they understood the words they were reading, or to give an intelligent account of what had been recently the subject of their lessons.

Some progress in writing, arithmetic, geography, musical notation, rectilinear drawing and grammar was being made, but

> the attainments in the respective classes were very indifferent; the first class being only able to read simple narratives, and that without accuracy or apparent intelligence . . . The remaining four classes were in a state of great backwardness, partly owing, it was said, to irregularity of attendance.

From 1840, in fact, the inspectors began to report critically on the work of the monitorial schools. The Rev. Baptist W. Noel, not an inspector but employed by the Committee of Council in the summer of 1840 to visit schools in Birmingham, Manchester, Liverpool and elsewhere in Lancashire, reported that 'the great majority of the patrons and conductors of the national and Lancasterian schools which I visited only profess to teach the children reading, writing, and arithmetic'. He found that their knowledge of anything else (including the

E

geographical whereabouts of Lancashire or Liverpool) was non-existent, but also that, 'unhappily, many of the schools were very unsuccessful in teaching what they profess to teach'. His general summary is not untypical of the reports which were now being submitted on both British and National schools:

> In some of the girls' schools very few of the children could write, and the writing was very bad; while even in the boys' schools, where more attention is paid to this important art, there were very few boys, and in very few schools, who had attained to a good running-hand without the aid of lines. In several of the girls' schools the children do not learn arithmetic at all. The masters of the boys' schools always profess to teach it, but I found the boys sometimes exceedingly defective in their knowledge of even the earliest and simplest rules. In one national school in a large town and a populous neighbourhood I found only six boys capable of working a short sum in simple multiplication, and five out of the six brought a wrong answer. In another, where 167 persons where present, I found only 12 who professed to understand compound addition: and when I set these a sum in simple multiplication to work separately, one of the 12 brought a right answer . . . But it was in their understanding of the Scriptures, daily read, that I regretted to find the most advanced children of the national schools so extremely defective.

Of the National schools he had visited he wrote that 'on the moral and religious training in these schools, I can say very little. In almost all the schools which I examined on this point there was scarcely any such thing.'[17]

There is no doubt that the Kennington Schools were of a much higher standard and greatly more efficient than the ones described in Lancashire – the result, it would seem, of the interest shown by the committee and the quality of the teachers they had sought and obtained. The position at Norwich, however, must raise some doubts about the level of attainment possible even in a good National school. If, with enlightened superintendence, a wide curriculum, apparatus, and the advantages of a centralised arrangement for training suitable monitors, what was achieved at the Norwich school was so indifferent, it is unlikely that the achievement at Kennington can have been very much better. Since the targets set throughout the monitorial system were so modest, it was no doubt easy to be sanguine about modest results.

At Kennington the children's attainments were displayed with some pride. The supporters of the schools were frequently invited either to attend a public examination of the children or to visit the schools. A notice of a sermon in May 1827 on behalf of the schools also announced such a public examination (held, it should be noted, on a Sunday):

On SUNDAY, 27th MAY, 1827, TWO SERMONS

Kennington National Schools.

On Sunday Next, the 20th of May, 1827,

At Two o'clock in the Afternoon,

A PUBLIC EXAMINATION

OF THE

CHILDREN BELONGING to the ABOVE SCHOOLS,

WILL TAKE PLACE

At the School-Rooms in the Kennington Oval

AND

On Sunday, the 27th May, 1827,

TWO SERMONS

WILL BE PREACHED AT

ST. MARK's CHURCH, KENNINGTON, FOR THE BENEFIT OF THESE SCHOOLS.

THAT IN THE MORNING

By the Rt. Rev. Father in God, Christopher, Lord Bishop of Gloucester

THAT IN THE EVENING

By the Rev. John R. Pitman, A.M.

Alternate Morning Preacher at Belgrave and Berkeley Chapels; and
Alternate Evening Preacher at the Foundling and Magdalen Hospitals.

*Divine Service will commence at Eleven o'Clock in the Morning; And at
Half-past Six o'Clock in the Evening.*

The Subscribers and Friends to these Schools are respectfully invited
to attend at the Examination, in order to satisfy themselves that the Instruction, Conduct, and Appearance of the Children are such as to merit
a continuance of their Support.

A report of this examination held on 20 May 1827 tells of the
'first classes' in the two schools (thirty-two boys and thirty-six
girls) being 'severally examined by the Revd Mr. Otter, and the
Revd Mr. Edwards, in the presence of a number of visitors'.
The result of the examination was said to be satisfactory (as it
normally was in all these reports). The one occasion when the
content of the public examination is revealed is in a manuscript
'programme for the examination on Sunday the 23rd May 1830',
which reads:

Reading, – questions and spelling	$\frac{1}{2}$ hour
Catechismal questions	$\frac{1}{4}$
Tables	$\frac{1}{4}$
Prayers and singing (in conclusion)	$\frac{1}{4}$
Total	$1\frac{1}{4}$ hours

There is no doubt that some effort was made at Kennington – at least by the late 1830s – to encourage something more
than the simple routines. A passage in Richard Cannon's report
to the 1838 annual meeting is the first clear indication of this:

The committee continue to avail themselves of the improvements, which are suggested from time to time in the
National system of education, by introducing such books,
maps, &c, as are considered to encrease in the children a
desire for useful and religious knowledge, and to induce

them to believe, that their school-hours are, as it is really intended, times of active amusement and instruction, and not of restriction and punishment.

That the committee in general agreed with this philosophy of education as including 'active amusement' was confirmed a year later when a printed statement was issued inviting 'parents of families of the labouring classes, resident in or near the district of Kennington' to send their children to the schools for a 'religious and useful education'. Even in a statement of this kind, published over the names of the minister and assistant minister of St Mark's and Richard Cannon, it was considered important to include the following as one of the five short paragraphs it contained:

> With this view the Kennington National Schools are founded; – proper regulations are laid down for the management of them; – the lessons of instruction for each of the school-hours are so varied as to keep the attention of the children constantly on the alert, and to afford amusement as well as information.

The same phrase, 'amusement as well as information', was being used fifteen years later: in 1854, five months after Cannon's resignation from the committee, a notice of a sermon contained the following:

> The children are instructed in reading, writing, and arithmetic. The Holy Scriptures are read every day, and form a specific lesson in each class. The lessons of instruction for each of the school-hours are varied so as to keep the attention of the children constantly on the alert, and to afford amusement as well as information on subjects which will be useful to them in future life.

The National Society itself, in its first report, commented that 'the happiness of the children under this plan of education forms a prominent subject of remark'.[18] It is not possible to say to what extent the happiness of the children featured in the interests of the National schools themselves, as well as in the philosophy of the national committee. Nor is it possible to say how far the precepts at Kennington were carried out in practice, but it is obvious from the continued use of these phrases over so long a period of time that the precepts were of importance to the Kennington committee.

Richard Cannon's reference to 'books, maps, &c' is one of the few clues to the possibility that equipment and aids were obtained – as at Norwich – to interest the children. The existence of equipment has never, of course, meant that it is used. One of H.M. Inspectors, reporting on the Midland District in 1845, after Committee of Council grants for the purchase of apparatus had become available, described how teaching could be 'beguiled of many of its discouragements' when a master went to the cupboard and brought out 'a new globe, or, perhaps, the roll of music-sheets, or the measuring chain, or mechanical model, which are the pride of his heart, and one of the glories of his school'. How rare this was, however, is illustrated from the same inspector's reports on individual schools, where apparatus is rarely mentioned, except to refer to the lack of it. On one page, for example, he mentions an infant school in Birmingham and a school at Great Bowden, at both of which 'apparatus is much wanted'. At a school taught by a mistress at Blackfordby there was 'an excellent collection of apparatus of which she does not understand the use'.[19]

At Kennington there are only two references to purchases other than books in the period up to 1840. The first is in the 1836 annual report, which stated that the committee had, 'in accordance with the wish of the subscribers . . . introduced additional books of instruction, as well as *maps*, for the use of the respective schools'. The second is Cannon's reference to maps, quoted above. References to the purchase, and in some cases donation, of books are frequent, from the very beginning. In the period 1824–6 the sum of £42.1s.11d. was spent on 'books, slates, and other articles necessary for the instruction of the children'. In 1827 books and stationery cost £9.11s.9d. In 1834 the committee decided 'that the introduction of particular books of moral instruction, and useful exercises, histories, &c, be, in addition to the Bible and other religious books, now used in the schools, be also taken into consideration at some special meeting of the subscribers'. At a meeting of the committee in 1839, 'six dozen New Testaments, and fifty Trimmers Abridgments[20] were decided to be supplied for the use of the two schools'.

Books, especially Bibles, were also sometimes given as

rewards to children, particularly on leaving school. In 1828 the master and mistress of the schools were instructed by the committee to report the names of boys and girls who were leaving 'after completing the usual course of education . . . in order that the committee may present such boy, or girl, with a Bible, Testament, or Prayer-book'. Six years later the annual meeting empowered the committee to give 'Bibles, Testaments, or Prayer-books, to such boys and girls, as quit the schools and evince a desire of profiting by and keeping up the instruction and good habits which they acquired at school'. No explanation for re-opening the subject is offered, but it may be that a new stress was now being laid not on the indiscriminate distribution of books, but on their use as rewards for past efforts and good intentions.

Rewards and punishments were, as we have seen, features of the monitorial system in general. The early Kennington records show nothing of the forms of punishment used, but it is probable that the schools adopted the methods widely in use in National schools – shaming children in various ways before the school and keeping them in after school (and, as we shall see, expulsion). Corporal punishment would not have fitted in with the general outlook of the committee; there is no evidence of corporal punishment being used or sanctioned, and indeed there is no such evidence until the 1880s. This does not amount to proof that there was no corporal punishment in earlier decades of the schools' existence, but it is important to emphasise the strong opposition to corporal punishment in the two societies in the early nineteenth century. Lancaster evolved a complex and often bewildering system of punishments; although some of them appear to us cruel (for example, shutting children in cupboards and hoisting them to the ceiling in baskets) they did not include the infliction of corporal pain. The atmosphere in the National Society was hostile to corporal punishment. A discussion took place on the committee of the Westminster Free School, for example, on the subject of corporal punishment and 'the committee were decidedly of opinion as the same was not sanctioned by the Madras system, it ought not on any account to be permitted'. A minute of the National Society's school committee to this effect was read to the master and mistress 'as a guide for their conduct in this respect'.[21] The master in charge of the central school at Baldwin's Gardens

was, in fact, dismissed in 1827, for 'severe personal chastise-
ment' of a boy, in spite of his apologies.[22]

The rewards at Kennington concerned mainly the payment
of monitors, and their payment was in fact described as a
reward (in 1836, for instance, 'the following sums were authorised
to be distributed as rewards to the teachers and assistant
teachers . . . '). The accounts contain frequent mention of
rewards; in 1827, for example, there is an item of expenditure
of £3.14s.6d. for 'clothes, given as rewards to certain boys', and
the following year there is an item of £2.17s.7d. for 'rewards to
children after examination'. In 1836 expenditure of £12.10s.11d.
was incurred for 'rewards to the children, including articles of
clothing for 30 girls'. It had been the intention of the committee
from the beginning to 'supply clothing to a portion of the
children, as an encouragement for regularity and good conduct,
and a reward to the most deserving'. In 1837 the committee
reported on the working of the scheme – showing that the
clothing was still for Sunday wear only:

BOYS' SCHOOL, KENNINGTON OVAL,
25th MAY, 1837.

The *Committee* of the *Kennington District Schools*, with a view to
the Encouragement of Good Conduct, and to the Excitement of
Emulation, have caused certain Articles of Clothing, consisting of
Caps, Jackets, and Waistcoats, to be distributed in the Boys'
School.

The *Boys* selected for these Rewards are to be recommended,
from time to time, by the Master, for the approval of the Committee, and are to consist of such as are punctual in their Attendance
at School and at Church,—attentive to their Learning,—clean in
their Persons and Dress,—respectful in their Behaviour,—and of
strictly Moral Conduct.

The *Parents* are to engage to return these Articles of Clothing
to the Master, on each Monday Morning, after being delivered
on Saturday for Wear on the Sunday at Church: They are to keep
the several Articles clean and in good order, and to furnish their
Children with other corresponding Articles of Clothing so as to
promote Neatness and Cleanliness.

The *Committee* require the Master to report, each Month, that
these Injunctions and Conditions are strictly fulfilled by the
Children as well as by their *Parents*.

By Direction of the Committee,
RICHARD CANNON,
Treasurer.

A separate scheme seems to have been inaugurated in 1832 to distribute charitable clothing to poor families in the district. The committee was no doubt responsible for promoting this scheme, but it was organised through the church:

St. Mark's, Kennington,
1st January 1832

Much benefit having been found to arise by the distribution of articles of clothing among the children of the
District Schools, particularly at this period of the year,
when the parents of many of them are suffering inconvenience and distress from the want of employment and
of the means of satisfying the increased wants of their
families; –
It is proposed,
    That a fund be raised, by moderate subscriptions from
the inhabitants of the district, for supplying stockings,
flannel, &c, to such children as shall be considered proper
objects for such charitable assistance . . .

An initial list of subscriptions (the largest, a guinea, from the Rev. Mr Otter) totalled £5.7s.0d. The school committee was acting as a supplementary agency to the church in charitable endeavours.

The aims of the elementary schools, as we have seen, were a mixture of social, moral, philanthropic and educational ones. A child who attended regularly at school and church, and observed the rules, was following the right moral path, and rewards were therefore socially and morally important. The presentation of Bibles to school leavers who had acquired 'good habits' was therefore as important as the incentives used during the course of instruction itself. On one occasion the committee showed that they believed that even after the child had left school their work was not over. In 1838 the committee let it be known that it was proposed 'when the state of the funds will admit, to give rewards to deserving boys and girls, who go from the school as servants in families, and who, after a certain period of service, shall obtain from their masters or mistresses a certificate of their good conduct and fidelity'. It is not known if the proposal was carried out, but the intention was still being expressed two years later (and indeed the National Society itself tried to encourage such contacts).[23]

Implicit in all of this discussion is the belief that in the late
1830s, as earlier in the century, the schools were an instrument
for attuning the children of the poor to the existing social
order. A statement for subscribers published by the Kennington
committee in 1837 re-affirmed that the system of instruction
at the schools, and the children's attendance at St Mark's
Church on Sundays, meant that 'the infant poor are thus
trained to habits of obedience and good order, and they acquire
that knowledge which is calculated to fit them for the stations
of life they may hereafter fill, and to enable them to become
good Christians, as well as useful and industrious members of
society'. The Rev. Baptist Noel, in his report on Lancashire
in 1840, explained that:[24]

> It would be a great mistake to point out to children
> instances of persons raised by successful industry, or by
> remarkable talent, to dignity and wealth, as
> illustrating what education may do for them. This, with
> respect to the greatest number who never can so rise,
> would form in them expectations which must be dis-
> appointed. What is worse, it would give them false views
> of a life of labour.

Education was by this period becoming more and more explicitly
defined as a factor in achieving social stability. Industrial
England was witnessing an increasing scale of social conflict.
In the period following the Napoleonic wars had come radical
organisation and agitation, followed later by the strains of the
period around the first parliamentary reform act of 1832, the
mushrooming of Owenite organisations (including trade unions)
in 1833 and 1834, and the appearance of Chartism and its
nation-wide campaigns from 1837. The momentum of political
and social change was considerable, and education had become accepted as a necessary barrier not only, as previously,
to crime and pauperism, but increasingly to social and political
disorder.

Teachers

The subscribers, committee and ministers of St Mark's Church
took a constant, detailed interest in the work of the two schools.
How much freedom was given to the master and mistress

within the school rooms at Kennington it is not possible to say, but it is obvious that throughout this period the teachers were operating a fixed system, and had little room for individual initiative within it. The dominant social purpose of the school also meant that the control of the committee over what went on in the schools was total, and that the teacher here, as in all such schools, was obliged to do precisely what the committee and the minister considered necessary. The master and mistress, it is important to note, had to come up for re-appointment annually by the general meeting of subscribers. The teachers could not have had any educational objectives other than those fixed for them by the committee, the subscribers and the ministers of the church. One positive outcome of this situation was that constant interest by relatively enlightened patrons (which the Kennington ones certainly were) could make for reasonably high and stable standards, in an age when the level of competence reached by and expected of teachers was low.

Nothing is known about the previous experience of the first teachers appointed at Kennington, except that Mr Hitchen was recommended – and almost certainly, therefore, trained – by the National Society. The Society's Central School in Baldwin's Gardens (it moved to Westminster in 1832) provided courses of training which at the beginning of this period normally lasted for two months, during which time half a guinea or a guinea a week was paid 'according to behaviour', and at the end of which a gratuity of five guineas was paid. By 1833 the training was averaging five months (which was much longer than that given by the British Society).[25] The National Society forbade teachers trained by them to depart from 'the beautiful and efficient simplicity of the system';[26] teacher training in a sense wider than simply learning how to apply a few fixed routines did not begin to develop until the 1840s. In a sample of thirty-eight schools surveyed in Lancashire, Cheshire and Derbyshire in 1840, seventeen teachers were shown as having had no 'instruction in the art of teaching', one had 'attended a school for about a fortnight', one had been trained for six weeks, and the rest had all had some such instruction but there is no indication of how much.[27] The quality of teachers, trained and untrained, in National and British schools varied enormously. The inspectors' reports from 1840 reflect this situation, as is shown by the following three items, adjacent in the same report of 1845:[28]

Antrobus	A very neat little village school-house in which I found assembled 75 children: the boys taught by an infirm old man, who, having for many years kept a school in the parish, has been appointed to his present office, lest the new school should deprive him of his livelihood ...
Astbury	... Nothing can be more complete than the ignorance of the boys in everything, except reading, which the master has taught to them (mechanically) with great care, and which is all probably that he is competent to teach them.
Atherstone	... The master fills also the office of organist in the church. The moral ascendancy which he exercises in the school is highly creditable to his skill as a teacher.

Given the eager interest taken by the committee in the Kennington Schools, and the absence of any serious complaint about the teachers, it is fairly certain that Isaac Hitchen and Rebecca Marchant were teachers whose 'moral ascendancy' and other qualities were also 'highly creditable'.

Both these teachers remained at the school for a long period, Rebecca Marchant retiring in 1848 and Hitchen in 1842. The master's salary is given as £90 a year from 1828, and that of the mistress remained at £50 per year (the latter in some years receiving a gratuity of £5.5s. for extra needlework). In 1827 the following item appears in the committee's minutes:

The committee, being satisfied with the conduct and management of the respective schools, resolve, that a gratuity of five pounds be given to the master; – and the same sum as in the last year to the mistress, – as a testimony of their approbation: – But in reference to the letter recently received from the school-master, this committee desire it may be understood and explained to him, that they will not in future entertain any applications from him on the subject of salary or gratuity.

In 1838 it was agreed by the committee to pay a gratuity of two pounds per quarter to Miriam Marchant, Miss Marchant's niece, who lived with her, 'for her services as an assistant in the girls' school', but two years later it was decided 'that the assistant in the girls' school be discontinued'. When Miss Marchant retired her niece was appointed to act in her place. In 1832 the committee proposed and the general meeting agreed that Hitchen should be appointed collector of the subscriptions for the schools, and that he would be given 5 per cent of the sums he collected. It was not uncommon for teachers to supplement their income in one way or another – for example, by working as a clerk, shoemaker, handloom weaver or dressmaker.

The position of the Kennington schoolmaster and school-mistress, by comparison with those in other National schools in Lambeth can be seen from the tables drawn up by the treasurer in 1829, in an attempt to persuade the National Society to encourage standard rates of pay based on numbers of children (see Tables 6 and 7).

The housing built at Kennington was obviously generous by comparison with the other schools, and free coal was the accepted rule (5 chaldrons for the Kennington schoolmistress).

The two teachers were evidently able to conduct their schools in a manner which met with the approval of the committee. The draft of the first committee report in 1827 alluded to the good conduct of the children, 'indicating good and proper management on the part of the master and mistress' (altered in the published version to – 'the master and mistress are attentive and competent to their duties'). The minutes of a committee meeting at the end of the same year recorded that:

> It must always be borne in mind, that a *peculiar* excellence which prevails in conducting these schools on the approved National system, and which has gained for them, and still retains, many subscribers, consists of the mild, steady, and uniform mode of treatment of the children, without having recourse to harshness or severity of punishment, except in cases of crimes.

In 1832 the annual report paid a public tribute to the heads of the two schools:

> The master and mistress continue diligent and strict in the performance of their duties without having recourse to

Table 6

1st. July 1829

Statement showing the salaries, gratuities, and allowances, to the masters and mistresses of the several parochial and district schools in the Parish of Lambeth.

	Boys' Schools			No. of children on the school books	Average number in attend-ance
	Salary of master	Gratuity	Allowances		
	£ s d				
Lambeth	100 . .	none	House— rooms & kitchen Coals— 5 chal'n	380	330
Kennington	90 . .	none	House 5 rooms & kitchen Coals	180	136
Brixton	78 . .	none	House 2 rooms & kitchen Coals	164	140
Stockwell	78 . .	£5.5.– three times during a service of fourteen years	House 2 rooms & kitchen Coals	160	130
Waterloo	60 . .	10.–.–	House rooms & kitchen	280	230
Nine Elms Norwood					

harshness or severity: the appearance, regularity, and good order of the children, are the best proofs of the care and attention to their instruction.

Only rarely are there reports of the teachers having recourse to the committee to solve disciplinary problems, as in 1834 when the committee ordered a boy to be expelled 'for a flagrant act of insubordination'. The committee, as we have seen, itself dealt with problems of persistent absence. Conduct in the schools is invariably reported in the minutes to have been good, and only on a small number of occasions is there a glimpse of the

Table 7

			Girls' Schools in the Parish of Lambeth		
	Salary of mistress	Gratuity	Allowances &c.	No. of children on the school books	Average number in attend- ance
Lambeth					
Kennington	50.-.-	5.5.- in cons- ideration of extra labour in needle work	House— 4 rooms & kitchen Coals— about 5 chald'n	148	105
Brixton	50.-.-	none	House— 2 rooms & kitchen Coals	110	85 to 90
Stockwell	50.-.-	none	House— 2 rooms & kitchen Coals	116	100
Waterloo	40.-.-	10.-.-	House rooms & kitchen	160	120
Norwood					

school problems which the teachers had to face. The conduct of the boys, to take a rare example from 1831, was reported to have been good 'with the exception of William Ginn, whose mother attended, and represented him to be a most incorrigibly bad boy, but that she had <u>fortunately</u> succeeded in obtaining some temporary employment for him, which <u>fortunately</u> removes his pernicious example from the school'. Underlining was a common enough habit in the nineteenth century, but the two examples of it here are indication enough of the relief felt all round. On one occasion the committee called in the mistress to express dissatisfaction with the attendance of the girls at church, and on one occasion, in 1829, a special committee meeting was called to enquire 'into certain reports, which had been circulated, reflecting upon the conduct and character of the mistress of the girls' school'. This latter episode provides the only real 'human interest' story in these early records.

Although the four-page report of this meeting begins with a reference to reports that Miss Marchant was 'intemperate and violent in her conduct towards the children in the exercise of her duties', no further reference is made to this allegation in the report, and the meeting was obviously preoccupied with other matters. The main purpose of the meeting was to discuss reports that

> she was frequently absent from her house in the evening,
> – not returning home until a late hour, – and on some
> occasions, was absent the whole night, leaving the house in
> the charge of little girls, who are too young for such a trust,
> and who, for obvious reasons, ought not to be left in such
> a situation by themselves at night.

(If Miriam was living with her aunt at this time she would have been about five years old, and the 'little girls' in charge might have been baby-sitters.) The climax of the indictment was that

> on a recent occasion, she had staid out until a late hour,
> when on her return home she found the outer gates locked
> (as is the order of the committee) and that she had recourse
> to getting over the railing or wall, in order to gain
> admittance to her house.

Miss Marchant's explanations – which are not reported – seem
to have satisfied the committee, which decided unanimously
that 'no criminality can be attached to the mistress, as arising
out of this enquiry', which was described as having become
indispensable 'as well for the protection and defence of her
character, as for preventing the interests of the school from
being injured'. Although the committee felt 'much satisfaction
in relieving her from the charges imputed to her' and expressed
their willingness 'on every proper occasion, to protect and
support her', they had to urge her 'to observe great caution
and circumspection in all parts of her conduct'. She was not to
'leave her house *at night* in the charge of any of the school
girls; – nor shall she send any girl to a distant place out of the
district or parish, on business unconnected with the duties of
the schools'. The mistress promised the committee 'that when
she may have occasion to go out on an evening, she will return
at a reasonable hour, – and that she will take care to leave a
proper person in the temporary charge of her house'. This would
spare the committee the 'painful task' of having to enquire
into circumstances

> the details of which could only be obtained through the
> girls belonging to the school, or through other persons, to
> whom the committee do not wish to refer for information
> as to the proceedings of their school-mistress, whose conduct
> should be such as to prevent any cause of suspicion or
> distrust.

The committee (to use the phrase which they had used of their
teachers) were no doubt 'diligent and strict in the performance
of their duties without having recourse to harshness or severity'.
Rebecca Marchant was to continue as schoolmistress at Kennington for almost twenty years after this event, with no
further recorded incidents to trouble the waters.

About Isaac Hitchen there is nothing recorded at all, and
the committee's minutes for the period including his departure
have not been preserved. The accounts, however, show for
September 1842 a 'gratuity to Mr. Isaac Hitchen as a testimonial
of his faithful services as master for 18 years ... £10.10s.';
this is the only reference to his leaving the school, but there
is later evidence that his successor, Mr Hay, was in fact

F

appointed in this year. In July 1844, however, there is a remarkable entry in the accounts:

> To amount of collections after two sermons at St. Mark's Church, on Sunday 14th July –
> morning, by the Ven'ble Archdeacon Hoare, M.A.
>
> £29.7s.6d.
>
> evening, by the Revd. Isaac Hitchen, M.A.
>
> £15.

The sermon was preached not by Hitchen himself, after going through a rapid transformation which would have been impossible in nineteenth-century conditions, but by his son. The younger Isaac was born in 1816 (eight years before his father's appointment at Kennington), and was admitted as a pensioner at Pembroke College, Cambridge, in 1834. There is no information about who paid his fees. He received his M.A. in 1841, after being ordained the previous year. In 1844, when he preached this sermon, he was living in Glasgow as a private schoolmaster.[29] It would be interesting to know more about the educational background of Mr Hitchen and about that of his son – as interesting as it would be to know why Miss Marchant climbed the railings.

Notes

A bound volume of minutes and other documents, printed and manuscript, 1823–40.

A bound volume of receipts and accounts and other documents, 1824–46.

Minute book and correspondence, 1854–6.

Bundle of miscellaneous documents referring to St Mark's School in the mid-nineteenth century.

1 Thomas Bernard, Preface to *Of the Education of the Poor* (London, 1809), pp. 19–20.
2 *Ibid.*, pp. 27–8.
3 'Standing Rules and Regulations', *First Annual Report of the National Society* (London, 1812), p. 37.
4 Pamela C. Lewis, 'The Early Charity Schools and National Schools of Tooting and Streatham', p. 32.
5 M. E. Sadler and J. W. Edwards, 'Summary of Statistics, Regulations, &c., of Elementary Education in England and Wales. 1833–1870', *Special Reports on Educational Subjects*, ii, p. 16.
6 *Ibid.*, p. 17.
7 *Minutes of the Committee of Council on Education, 1845* (London, 1846), i, p. 179.
8 *Ibid., 1840–41* (London, 1841), pp. 374–5.

9 *Thirteenth Annual Report of the Society for the Encouragement of Parochial Schools in the Diocese of Durham and Hexhamshire* (Durham, 1824), pp. 20, 24.

10 *Census, 1851*, pp. xxxix–xl. This point is also discussed, in relation to the 1834 Select Committee, in George C. T. Bartley, *The Schools for the People*, p. 55.

11 A. E. Dobbs, *Education and Social Movements 1700–1850*, p. 152. Our attention was drawn to this passage by a reference in A. F. B. Roberts, 'A New View of the Infant School Movement', p. 157.

12 For a discussion of this topic see R. Szreter, 'The Origins of Full-time Compulsory Education at Five', pp. 16–28.

13 *Second Annual Report of the National Society* (1813), pp. 195–6.

14 *Thirty-fourth Annual Report of the National Society* (1845), inset.

15 Quoted from E. T. Davies, *Monmouthshire Schools and Education to 1870*, pp. 72–3.

16 *Minutes of the Committee of Council on Education 1840–41*, pp. 431–2.

17 *Ibid.*, pp. 174–5.

18 *First Annual Report of the National Society*, p. 56.

19 *Minutes of the Committee of Council on Education 1845*, I, pp. 240, 287.

20 Abridgments of the Old and New Testaments by Mrs Sarah Trimmer were popular in schools for the poor from the 1780s.

21 H. J. Burgess, 'The Educational History of the National Society 1811–1833', p. 213.

22 H. J. Burgess and P. A. Welsby, *A Short History of the National Society 1811–1961*, p. 9.

23 *Ibid.*, p. 6.

24 *Minutes of the Committee of Council on Education 1840–41*, p. 167.

25 H. J. Burgess, *Enterprise in Education*, p. 52; Sadler and Edwards, 'Summary of Statistics', p. 16.

26 R. W. Rich, *The Training of Teachers in England and Wales during the Nineteenth Century*, p. 2.

27 *Minutes of the Committee of Council on Education 1840–41*, pp. 384–95.

28 *Ibid. 1845*, I, p. 279.

29 J. A. Venn, *Alumni Cantabrigiensis*, pt II, 1752–1900, III (London, 1947), p. 386.

Chapter four

Achievement and crisis 1840-60

Nationally, the period from the 1830s saw the beginning of state involvement in education. The first government grants in aid were channelled through the National and British Societies from 1833. In 1839, against opposition from the Church of England, the government created a Committee of the Privy Council to deal with educational matters, including the distribution of grants for school building. At the same time the first of Her Majesty's Inspectors were appointed, and the Church won the concession that no inspector of National schools would be appointed without the prior approval of the Archbishops of Canterbury and York. A Committee of Council Minute of 1846 introduced the pupil teacher system, under which apprentices would be paid out of government funds. They had to be at least thirteen when they were appointed, they would serve for five years and would then be able to compete for Queen's Scholarships. These entitled successful candidates to up to three years of training at the colleges which were being established by the religious denominations. Those who did not wish to be apprentices were able to continue as 'stipendiary monitors' (earning £5–£12.10s. per year) up to the age of seventeen.[1] This was the beginning of the end of the monitorial system.

The National Society remained by far the largest body which provided schools, and received by far the largest share of the government's annual grants (which from 1843 also became available to purchase equipment and furniture, as well as to build schools). In 1846–7 there were almost a million children in the National Society's 17,000 daily schools (still counting boys' and girls' departments as separate schools).[2] Problems of attendance remained acute, the average length of school life remained short, and disputes about the possibility of establishing a comprehensive, national system of elementary education remained clamorous in the 1840s and 1850s. The number of schools sponsored by the Church of England, mainly through the National Society, and by the nonconformists, mainly through the British Society but also through denominational bodies (for example, Wesleyan and Independent) was increasing. The numbers of children in the schools were also increasing, but the provision was inadequate in some, especially industrial, areas; the quality of the schooling was frequently low; teachers were ill-prepared or unprepared; fluctuating attendance reduced the efficiency of what the schools could do. In the census of education conducted in 1851 by Horace Mann he examined the question of why something like a million children between the ages of five and twelve were in receipt of no education at all. He considered that there were on paper enough school places, but very often these were out of reach of those requiring education, and therefore worthless; but it was also often the case that 'where great numbers of children live from day to day without instruction, they have actually in the very midst of them an ample school provision'. He believed that where fees were charged, poverty rarely accounted for children's absence – it was 'a hindrance less resulting from the want of means than from the want of inclination', though he conceded that there were large numbers of destitute children 'who, having either lost their parents or been cast by them adrift, perpetually haunt large towns and cities, snatching a miserable and precarious subsistence as the fruit of vagrancy or crime'. The labouring classes, he concluded, were frequently uninterested in education, because they could see no benefit in it: they had been conditioned to see themselves in a 'station' in life to which the available schooling seemed irrelevant. The attitude is summarised in this crucial passage:[3]

It is hardly, therefore, matter for surprise, although undoubtedly it is for lamentation, that the working classes – seeing that the purely mental training which their children pass through in the present class of schools can rarely exercise an influence upon their future temporal prosperity, and having for some generations past been tutored not to look *beyond their station* – should esteem a thorough education of this character to be not worth the time and money needful for its acquisition. More, they may conceive, of *useful* information – useful to their children in their probable employments – may be learnt outside the school than in it.

In the 1840s there were various plans for a national system of education which would improve the supply. The 1846 pupil teacher scheme was designed to improve the teaching and the efficiency of the schools. The 'ragged schools' which began to come into existence from the mid-1840s were aimed at the most destitute and vagrant children, frequently offering them food and shelter as much as any kind of education. In addition to other regular day and Sunday schools in existence in Lambeth in 1851 there was a ragged school (opened in that year) not far from the Kennington Schools,[4] and there was also a White Cottage School House which was used 'on weekday evenings as a Ragged School and also as a Working Mans Institute'.[5]

The general condition of the Kennington Schools at this period can be judged from the inspector's reports, particularly on the girls' school. In 1848 the H.M.I. declined to make any comment, as Rebecca Marchant had only just resigned and her niece had taken over for a probationary period. The following year his report was favourable, but Maria Marchant was weak in methodical teaching and was advised to 'study a good manual'. In 1850 the discipline was found to be improved, and the children 'neat, clean, and orderly behaved'; the school would benefit from 'the more competent provision of books and maps, which the managers propose to furnish'. The H.M.I. visited the school unexpectedly in 1852 and found the children as neat and 'orderly behaved' as ever, even though Miss Marchant had had to 'contend with serious disadvantages arising from her own ill-health'. Presumably for this reason, there was a change of mistress by the following year, the new mistress being the wife of Mr Hay, the master of the boys' school since Hitchen's resignation. The school was said to be suffering from the inevitable disturbance accompanying the change of mistress. The report for 1855 gives the fullest account of the school in this period:

> Boys. School-room as before; wood floor; offices, good: play ground, a garden well employed; residence, good. Desks, parallel enough. Registers (Mr. Hay's) duly kept.
> Apparatus sufficient, Discipline good. Instruction fair.
> Fitness for training apprentices, good.

Continues in an efficient condition, and conducted with great professional zeal.

Girls. School-room, as before, wood floor, offices good: residence, good. Not enough humble books. Registers (Hay's) duly kept. Apparatus enough. Discipline and instruction fair. Fitness for training apprentices, good.

The master exercises considerable influence in the conducting of this school which is under excellent auspices and exhibits fair discipline and attainment. Industrial work suitably cultivated.

Continues entitled to the same favourable record as last year.

The same H.M.I. had two years before also expressed his admiration for the 'excellent auspices': he had noted on a letter from the Committee of Council that the school was 'of so much local importance and under such zealous management'. These were as decided votes of confidence as could be imagined.

The pupil teacher scheme introduced in 1846 was obviously also working well. In 1853, for example, there was a total of eight such apprentices in the two schools. A note accompanying the grant to pupil teachers in that year pointed out that 'Cavill spells incorrectly. Bayley, Langridge, and Bruce should pay attention to grammar.'

> *Committee of Council on Education,*
> *Privy Council Office, Downing Street,*
> *4th January 1853*

Kennington Oval Nat^l. School.

SIR,

THE Lord President of the Council, having had under consideration the Report of Her Majesty's Inspector, has authorized payment from the Parliamentary Grant for Education, in accordance with the particulars set forth in the annexed Schedule.

Post Office Orders to the amount of £171.13.4 to provide for these payments, are herewith transmitted to you.

The Christian Names of the Payees are omitted in the Schedule, for the sake of security in transmission, but they must be given at full length at the Post Office to obtain payment of the Orders.

Care should be taken that the Post Office Orders be delivered to the several persons as they are numbered in the Schedule; the Number being the only means of distinguishing one Order from another, when the amounts are the same.

The Signatures of the several persons should be affixed in full in the first column of the Schedule, upon the receipt of the Order or Orders appropriated to them; and the Schedule itself, detached from this Letter, should be returned to the Committee of Council by the next Post.

Upon presenting Orders at the Post Office for payment, Pupil Teachers should be accompanied by one of their Parents, or, in the case of Orphans, by their natural Guardian; and the Instructions printed on the Orders should be carefully followed.

I beg leave to request your careful attention to the enclosed document concerning QUEEN'S SCHOLARSHIPS. *Perhaps, when you have perused it, you will be kind enough to circulate it among your Pupil Teachers, and otherwise make it known in your School. Another document is enclosed concerning the* APPRENTICESHIP OF ADDITIONAL PUPIL TEACHERS.

I am also to request that the following remarks may be communicated verbatim to the several persons whom they concern. Their Lordships' decisions upon the Grants of next year will proceed upon the assumption that this communication has been made.

Teachers who were certificated (that is, had passed an examination at the end of a full-time course of training, or as practising teachers had passed an external examination) were paid for their part in teaching pupil teachers ($1\frac{1}{2}$ hours, five days a week, before or after school hours), and Mr and Mrs Hay were clearly seen as suitable teacher-trainers. Mr Hay, it is worth noting, also attended classes under the Department of Science and Art (first founded as the Department of Practical Art in 1852 and re-formed with the new name in 1853); in 1856 the committee noted in its minutes that 'the Council of Science and Art Marlborough House have awarded to Mr. Hay the master as a geometrical prize a case of instruments'. In 1855, after fourteen years' service, Hay had applied to the committee for an increase in salary. When appointed in 1842 Hay's salary was fixed at £80 per year (£10 lower than Hitchen's had been), and it was now raised to £90.[6]

Pupil teachers, to qualify for grant, had to pass an annual examination by an H.M.I. If successful, the apprentices received a grant (£10 in the first year, rising by increments of £2.10s. a year to £20 in the last year). The master and mistress received an annual payment of £5 for one apprentice, £9 for two, £12 for three, and £3 for each one above three.[7] In 1851, on the night of the census, Miriam Marchant had staying with her two pupil teachers aged sixteen and seventeen (and one 'scholar' aged ten; at the Hays' there were also Mrs Hay's mother and a niece, and at the parsonage, in addition to Mr and Mrs Lane and their four children, there were their nurse, cook and house-maid, and Mrs Lane's sister, with her three children and two servants).[8]

Pupil teachers from Kennington were successful in obtaining Queen's Scholarships. In February 1853, for example, the chairman of the managers received the following notification from the secretary of the Committee of Council on Education:

> I have much pleasure in informing you that the Lord President of the Council has been pleased to award at the Winchester Training School a Queen's Scholarship of the amount of £20 for one year to George Tear recently examined at the Highbury Training School.

To be accepted by the Committee of Council as a pupil teacher a candidate had not only to pass the examination but also to sign a form of indenture. On only one occasion in the records did an apprentice, one Mary Hooker, cancel her indentures. She began as an apprentice in September 1853, and was admitted on the recommendation of the H.M.I. as a second-year pupil teacher, though with reservations on the part of the Committee of Council. At a special meeting of the Kennington committee in February 1855 Mrs Hooker applied to withdraw her daughter; she expressed Mary's grievances, which 'related more to the domestic management of the establishment than to the discipline of the school and her disappointment altogether in the position of her daughter, than to the instruction she had received as she expressed herself perfectly satisfied with the education imparted'. There is no explanation of the nature of the dispute, but the committee felt it advisable for the future 'that the relative duties between teacher and pupil be more regularly defined'. It took two meetings to complete the procedure for Mary's withdrawal, as permission had first to be sought from the Committee of Council. The reply agreeing to the cancellation of the indentures contained an implied rebuke for the school committee:

> In selecting any new candidates for apprenticeship my Lords trust that every care will be used in presenting only those girls for examination whose steadiness of character

and sense of duty appear to mark them out as likely to
entertain a higher regard than has been manifested by
Mary Hooker, of the obligations which they contract as
pupil teachers.

The committee was obviously anxious in this period to keep
the school in good repair and make it as efficient for its purposes
as possible. Even in January 1825, only a few months after the
boys' school had opened, the committee had had to spend
money on improvements. The schoolroom had been laid with
bricks, and as a result of 'its continued dampness, and of the
danger to be apprehended with respect to the health of the
children', it was immediately decided to replace the brick
flooring with boards. There is a full account written by Cannon
in 1840 of the problems of heating and ventilating the schoolrooms, questions which had not been adequately attended to
when the buildings were constructed. In winter the open coal
fires provided insufficient heating and in cold weather attendance was therefore poor and the children's 'application and
learning . . . had been much retarded'. In hot weather the slated
roofs had made the rooms 'scarcely supportable'. The 'recent
invention of Dr. Arnott's stoves for large rooms' had attracted
some members of the committee, and after due consideration
one such stove was installed in the girls' schoolroom, replacing
and stopping up the fireplace. This caused the room to be too
warm in moderate weather and the bad ventilation caused
drowsiness. The lack of an open fire also made it difficult to
dry the children's clothes in very wet weather. When a stove
was installed in the boys' room, therefore, the open fire-place
and chimney were retained, and a new outside chimney was
built to carry away the fumes from the stove. The girls' room
was adapted likewise and ventilators were made – two in the
roofs of each of the schoolrooms, and four in each schoolroom
floor, together with metal air-bricks in the outer walls of the
buildings. As a result, wrote Cannon, attendance was now
'greater than during former periods . . . the health and
general appearance of the children are in a very pleasing and
satisfactory state'. The National Society, it should be pointed
out, had from the early days paid much attention to questions
of space, ceiling height and ventilation. In 1816, for example,
the Society published a detailed report from its sub-committee

'appointed to prepare plans for building schools', with the intention of uniting 'the greatest possible convenience with the least possible expense'. The committee recommended seven square feet per child (the figure previously used had been six), various types of roofing and flooring – with preference for brick, ample lighting from windows placed very high, designs 'to prevent echo and much noise', doors which would 'introduce currents of air upon the children sitting near them as little as possible', and privies 'separate for the sexes, and so placed as not to become offensive'. It recommended heating 'most conveniently provided, and with least loss of room and interruption to business, by means of flues like those of a hot-house, or by Swedish or other brick stoves'. Ventilation singled out as 'an object of great importance', was discussed in some detail, with recommendations for the windows, the ceiling, apertures 'to allow the foul air to escape upward into the cavity of the roof' and out of it, with the apertures protected against snow, rain and severe cold by 'a contrivance resembling Venetian blinds'.[9] Whether or not Cannon and the committee were influenced by the standards suggested by the National Society is not known; their grasp of the importance of problems like ventilation came late, but once they understood what was at stake they made serious efforts to solve the problems effectively.

Average monthly attendance in January to March 1854 was between 80 and 83 per cent for the boys and 73 and 77 per cent for the girls. In June average attendance was 201 out of 249 boys on the books (81 per cent) and 137 out of 177 girls (77 per cent). Seasonal and other variations make comparison with the rather higher figures quoted earlier for the late 1830s somewhat meaningless; the important, if negative, point is that average attendance had not materially improved. From 1844 the children's weekly payments were raised to two pence a week (annual income from school pence ranged from £53 to £62 between 1840 and 1843; in the following two years it was £102 and £114).

The only occasion in this period when evidence has been found of the school applying for financial aid either to the National Society or to the Committee of Council occurred in 1844. The statistics of applications for aid from parliamentary grant in that year, published by the Committee of Council, show Kennington Oval National School as having applied for aid for 'adding class-rooms to the school'. The total estimated expenditure was £230, and the Committee of Council decided to grant £57.[10]

The accounts for this period indirectly point to some features of the life of the school. Children continued to be provided with clothes for Sunday wear: the 1844 accounts, for instance, mention 'clothing of 21 girls. Frocks, &c. 7. 14. 6. Bonnets. 2. 2. 0.'. There is regular mention of expenditure for refreshments for the children at the public examination (£3.15s.8d. in 1841), and occasionally for other events. In 1840, for example:

| 10th February | By amount of sums paid for refreshments, &c., distributed to the children on the occasion of the marriage of Her Majesty Queen Victoria | £5. 6s. 0d. |

and two years later:

| 25th January | By amount expended in buns, oranges, and wines among the children on the occasion of the christening of His Rl. Highness the Prince of Wales | £3. 17s. 0d. |

If the children all got buns, oranges and wine for the smaller sum, it would be interesting to know what the refreshments consisted of for the larger one! In the absence of any royal event in 1843 the committee spent £2. 2s. on framing a picture of Queen Victoria.

Other expenditure in the 1840s included regular amounts for Bibles, prayer books and other books, metal pens, copy-books and other stationery, and the needlework requisites for the girls' school:

| For articles used in instructing the children in needle-work; viz. canvas, – calico, – thread, and needles | £5. 9s. 11d. |

In 1840 it cost the committee £1.12s. to purchase iron pens, £6.2s.6d. for stationery and £2.10s. 'for emptying privies'. Expenditure in 1845 included fourteen new window-blinds (£2.7s.10d.) and 352 copy-books (£3.16s.).

By the end of this period holidays were beginning to be
longer than we have seen them so far. In 1858–9, for example,
as school pence receipts in Table 8 show, there was a four-week
summer holiday, two weeks at Christmas, a week at Easter
and a day or two at Whitsuntide.

The outstanding recorded events in the life of the school in
the 1850s were a financial crisis and the related departure of
Richard Cannon from the committee. In January 1854 Cannon
wrote a letter to the Rev. Charlton Lane beginning: 'Under
circumstances of a painful nature I am compelled to place in
your hands my resignation of the treasurership of the Kennington
Schools'. He went on to hope that the committee would believe
that he had always had the interests of the schools at heart.
'In the first year of my retirement from public life,' he continued,
'that I should be obliged to relinquish my connexion with the
Kennington Schools I deeply regret.' He hoped that the committee would 'put the most favorable construction on my
retirement'. This letter of resignation was put before a meeting
of subscribers nine days later. It was moved by Mr Young and
seconded by Mr Forest 'that the resignation be accepted'. It is
not clear whether, as one commentator suggests, Cannon's

Table 8

	Boys			
1858				
July 2	131	1	1	10
„ 9	Holidays			
„ 16	Holidays			
„ 23	Holidays			
„ 30	Holidays			
August 6	133	1	2	2
„ 13	170	1	8	4
„ 20	186	1	11	0
„ 27	185	1	10	10
Sept. 3	202	1	13	8
„ 10	205	1	14	2
„ 17	201	1	13	6
„ 24	207	1	14	6
		£13	10	—

offence was merely 'inefficiency, due to old age'. The finances, it is clear, were not in a good state. Between 1850 and 1853 Cannon was certainly still active, as we shall see when we discuss questions of drainage and cholera, which assumed importance locally in those years. It seems likely that Young and Robert Forest (the latter of whom had been on the committee of the schools with Cannon from the beginning and on the new parish vestry with him from 1825) played a leading part in forcing Cannon's resignation, and then took over as joint treasurers. Cannon may have been guilty of financial mismanagement; something in his private life may have proved unpalatable to the committee. Whatever happened, no expression of gratitude for Cannon's thirty years of enormous and dedicated work for the school was recorded, nor any other comment than 'that the resignation be accepted'. Cannon had been the pillar of the schools' 'zealous management'; in addition to donations, he had in the early days loaned the school (at no interest) a total of over £800, and for thirty years he had painstakingly kept the minutes and accounts, conducted the correspondence, and supervised the work of building and maintenance. He had been active in the affairs of the church and the parish. The fact that the subscribers, with Lane in the chair (and without Cannon present) accepted his resignation so ungraciously must indicate some more serious breach than can be explained merely by inefficiency.

There are dark hints, in fact, in the first paragraph of a statement put out by the new treasurers:

> The committee of the Kennington Schools are induced to call the serious consideration of the inhabitants of St. Marks, to the present state of the pecuniary affairs of the establishment: in so doing, it is with regret that they feel obliged to allude to the embarrassments of their late Treasurer, which to a certain extent have involved the schools in some difficulty, although the deficiency is not large, yet the debts which have been suffered to accumulate, together with the cost for improved drainage, in the aggregate amount to nearly the sum of £350.

As £138.17s.10d. of this debt was the cost of the new drainage, the deficiency was indeed 'not large'; the moral rather than the financial implications of Cannon's 'embarrassments' would seem to explain the treatment he received. The committee appealed for funds, and the debt was quickly liquidated. In response to an earlier appeal in connection with the drainage the Duchy of Cornwall had already promised a donation of £10, but this was raised to £25 when they learned of the difficulties partly due to 'the embarrassments of the late treasurer' (the phrase is repeated in the letter from the Duchy).

In 1861 the committee chairman was to inform subscribers that:

> one of the most liberal supporters of our parochial charities, has added to his other acts of beneficence, the purchase, from the Duchy of Cornwall, of the freehold of these schools, which he has settled in perpetuity, together with a handsome endowment, for the education of the poorer classes . . . in conformity with the regulations of the Committee of Council on Education, and according to the principles of the National Society.

The benefactor was, in fact, Robert Forest. The endowment brought in £60 per year, and it was just this sum, wrote H. H. Montgomery, Bishop of Tasmania and formerly Vicar of Kennington, later in the century, 'which enables us to carry on the schools without making them burdensome to the congregation'.[11] The purchase of the freehold cost £450, the endowment was for £1,000 (and he left a further £400 in his will).

Any change in the social composition of the schools could in this period have been only slight (if there was any change at all). The declared purposes of the schools, in fact, remained unchanged. At the beginning of this period (in September 1839) a joint appeal signed by the minister and assistant minister of St Mark's, the treasurer of the Kennington National Schools, and the treasurer of the infant and Sunday schools, described the schools as being 'for the purpose of training and instructing the children of the labouring classes, and of affording them the means, when of sufficient age to go forth into the world, of becoming useful members of the community, and of obtaining a livelihood for themselves by honest industry'. An accompanying report on the schools was designed to show 'that the general education and the religious interests of the labouring classes have been duly regarded by the supporters and managers of these institutions'. A report in 1846 described the advantages of the school's work to afford education 'to the children of the labouring classes'. Forest's deed of purchase of the freehold, dated November 1860, laid down that the schools were to be for 'the education of children and adults or children only of the laboring, manufacturing and other poorer classes in religion and useful knowledge'.

Notes

A bound volume of minutes and other documents, printed and manuscript, 1823–40.

Minute book and correspondence, 1854–6.

Visitors' book, 1854–64.

Bundle of miscellaneous documents referring to St Mark's School in the mid-nineteenth century.

Master's and Mistress' Report Book, 1863–95.

Book containing items requiring committee approval, 1863–95.

1 *Census, 1851*, p. xxxv.
2 *Ibid.*, p. lv; M. E. Sadler and J. W. Edwards, 'Summary of Statistics', *Special Reports on Educational Subjects*, ii, p. 26.
3 *Census, 1851*, pp. xl–xli.
4 Survey of London, xxiii, *South Bank and Vauxhall*, pt i, p. 142; Aileen Denise Nash, *Living in Lambeth 1086–1914*, p. 61.
5 Home Office, Census Papers: Ecclesiastical Returns (1851), H.O. 129, 31–7–1–7. Unfortunately none of the South London returns are extant for the education census.
6 Hay had, in fact, been attending classes of some kind since 1848. A document in the St Mark's file at the National Society mentions that he was attending evening classes in January of that year, and in July he is described as attending classes from 6.30 to 8.30 p.m. on Mondays and Thursdays, with examinations every other Saturday.
7 R. W. Rich, *The Training of Teachers in England and Wales during the Nineteenth Century*, pp. 119–22.
8 Lambeth Census 1851, Kennington 1st pt, H.O. 107 1573 2 3, p. 1, and H.O. 107 1053, p. 1.
9 *Fifth Annual Report of the National Society* (London, 1816), pp. 188–9. Appendix IV contains the full report.
10 *Minutes of the Committee of Council on Education, 1844*, i, pp. 286–9. A manuscript note in the St Mark's file at the National Society also refers to a grant of £59.10s. from the Committee of Council in 1865, and an application to the National Society in 1888 for help with an enlargement scheme. The next major improvement for which National Society help was given was in 1899.
11 H. H. Montgomery, *The History of Kennington and its Neighbourhood*, p. 137.

Chapter five

The Schools and the community to 1860

The parish of Lambeth continued to grow rapidly after the establishment of the Kennington Schools. At the national census in 1821 the total population of the parish was given as 57,638; at the 1851 census it had more than doubled, to 139,325. In the 1840s and 1850s there were oil, vitriol and wadding factories, and – from 1854 – a soap-making factory to add to the problems of smell, drainage and disease which were mounting in the area.[1] The poor rate was rising sharply (from nearly £33,000 in 1824 to nearly £77,000 thirty years later; though the numbers in the workhouse rose only slowly, the amount of weekly outdoor relief climbed from £194 in 1842 to £298 twelve years later).[2]

For the schools intended for the children of the poor (not only those of Kennington, but also others already in existence and being established in the parish), the population problem included one that affected London schools particularly acutely – the rapid turnover of families moving to be near employment, in a period before the cheap transport associated with buses and trams. The committee of the Kennington Schools expressed especial concern about this problem in 1838, when they included a commentary on it both in its report to the annual meeting, and in a statement on the schools which they submitted to the Archbishop of Canterbury. In the latter document they said:

> The frequent changes which take place among the children
> admitted into these and similar institutions in the several
> districts and parishes, may be ascribed, in a great degree,
> to the labouring classes of the community removing their
> residences according to the places, where they obtain
> employment. This is found to be the case in the Kennington
> district, and it is, without doubt, the same in other
> suburban districts, &c.

The committee told the annual meeting that this was dis-

G

heartening and irremediable, but that the National system
would continue to 'contend successfully' against the problem.

It is obvious from what has gone before that the majority of
children were from very poor families, that some went into
domestic service, and that church and school both saw their
role in the area as one of implanting moral order on social chaos.
The details of the children's social backgrounds, the employments of their parents and their own employments after they
left school are missing, but it is possible to catch a few glimpses
of the school in its environment.

There were inevitably problems when school broke up at
midday and in the afternoon. In 1829 the treasurer reported
to the committee that

> in order to remove the inconvenience and annoyance,
> arising to the immediate neighbourhood, in the dismissal
> of the children after school-hours, he had found it necessary
> to direct their being formed into four divisions, according
> to their places of residence, and to be dismissed at intervals,
> after being conducted to certain points under charge of the
> monitors of classes.

The arrangement, he later added, had succeeded in removing
'the evil, of which complaints have been frequently made'.
Over a quarter of a century later a neighbour of the schools
wrote to the committee, and his somewhat breathless letter is
worth reproducing in full:

> Renfrew Lodge, next the Oval
> Schools, Harleyford Road,
> 25th July 1856.

To the gentlemen
composing the committee

> I beg leave to address you, to complain of what has
> recently become an annoyance to me, and to suggest to
> you, the means of its removal.
>
> Some time since I remonstrated with the then school
> committee, (Mr. Cannon in particular) on the subject of the
> boys being turned into the street to play – accidents of a
> severe nature having thereby occurred; when the small
> railed in piece of ground just adjoining my house, was
> petitioned off, for a play ground; with a urinal next the

garden wall adjoining my house. Now this urinal, has been
at times exceedingly offensive and the boys, being restricted
to so small a ground, have at times made the proximity of
them, and their balls, any thing but agreeable; (as they get
on and over the present wall at pleasure). The remedy, I
respectfully submit would be in increasing the play ground;
and building a proper urinal, with a supply of water, and
raising the boundary wall and continuing it for about 18
feet (instead of the present open fence) adjoining my
garden.

On your referring to Mr. Hay, the school-master, he will
inform you that the school has the advantage of being
drained principally at my expense, which will be a saving
to its funds (the drainage cost me nearly £25.) and will, I
trust, operate with you, as some reason why I should not
be annoyed.

I have the honour to remain
Gentlemen
Yours respectfully
James Lovett Jones

At least we know that at this stage the children played with
balls, were cooped up in a small playground, climbed into the
neighbour's garden, and had a urinal without a supply of water.

Apart from this neighbour's view of the school there are no
other spectators' impressions. Bishop Montgomery, writing in
the 1880s gives a picture of the children at St Mark's Church
for the 11 a.m. service in the early decades of the schools'
existence:[3]

A few minutes before 11, the children from the Oval Schools
trooped into the porch and up the winding staircase towards
the belfry; and then through their own door, high up in
the wall of the organ. The boys and girls were dressed in
what is technically called 'clothing'; that is to say, in
uniform. The boys wore brown jackets and waistcoats, a
black tie and a regulation cap; their other garments were
according to the taste of their parents. The girls wore white
tippets, and sometimes they wore white caps.

On some occasions the children played a more conspicuous
part. At the services when sermons were preached on behalf

of the schools they were brought downstairs and stood under the gallery at the west end:

> The clerk gave out the hymn and then added, 'The hymn will be sung by the children alone.' This was meant to be a spur to the congregation when they passed the plate at the doors . . . Sometimes, again, an anthem was sung from the gallery by the girl or boy possessed of the best voice.

At other times, such as during Lent

> the Vicar ordered six boys and six girls to be brought downstairs: these, dressed in their 'clothing', were made to stand up on the free seats nearest the pulpit . . . and then the Vicar, Dr. Otter (afterwards Bishop of Chichester), put them through their Catechism, and asked them questions upon it for the benefit of the congregation.

At one of the first funerals in the vaults of the Church six boys 'went in procession from the house dressed in their "clothing"'.

By the 1850s the children were making other collective ventures out of the school, notably on Ascension Day. It is not clear when the practice began, but in 1854 the master reported to the committee that on Ascension Day 250 boys and 200 girls assembled at the schools and attended divine service at Kennington Church (as the average attendance at the schools at this time was 201 boys and 137 girls there were probably brothers and sisters present – the log books for the 1860s often report children absent to attend festivities at other schools). After the service the rest of the day was spent in the Oval cricket ground (it had become this in 1846), where the children 'were regaled in the afternoon with the usual fare of sandwiches, milk, buns, oranges, etc etc', and 'conducted themselves very orderly'. On the same occasion the following year the conduct of the children was described as 'correct and orderly'. The same applied when the master took thirty boys to the Crystal Palace, which had moved to Sydenham after the Great Exhibition of 1851, and to which children continued to be taken for special events (especially singing) in later decades. In 1866, for example, the committee approved 'Crystal Palace subscriptions' of five shilling each for the two schools and permission to take '80 boys on May day' and '30 girls to sing on May day'.

Apart from the fact that the 'plate' belonging to St Mark's

Church was hidden under the school floorboards during the anxieties that accompanied the great Chartist meeting on Kennington Common in April 1848, the only other demonstrable relationship between the school and the district is in connection with health.

Problems of public health became most dramatic in the 1830s and 1840s in relation to cholera epidemics. The first such epidemics came to England in 1831–2 and 1848–9, and it was in the knowledge of the imminent danger of the second epidemic that the Public Health Act of 1848 set up the General Board of Health and made possible the establishment of local boards. Local and metropolitan administration had not yet evolved to the point at which it could cope with serious problems of this kind – even if medical knowledge had been far enough advanced to understand the causes of this and other diseases. The fact that cholera was a water-borne disease was not known, but bad water supply and drainage were obvious enough causes of discomfort, unpleasantness and illness. In Lambeth attempts to combat cholera were, indeed, related to attempts to control sewage and prevent the flooding of the Effra Creek. The importance of this for the history of the Kennington Schools is that the battle for improved drainage, sewage and flood prevention was conducted over the names of the treasurer and chairman of their committee – Richard Cannon and Charlton Lane. In the early 1850s, in particular, Cannon and the school committee found themselves waging a public fight against the Metropolitan Commissioners of Sewers to get proper drainage and sewage in the whole neighbourhood. The committee's first objective, it said in a public statement in 1853, 'is to secure a continuance of the health of the children, as well as of the inhabitants of the neighbourhood in general'.

The schools, as we have previously seen, were built on a site which proved to be 'a perfect swamp of itself; – subject also to inundations from the adjoining creek and from high tides'. If the land had not been raised and drained (though in a rudimentary fashion) there were times when the children could not have attended school, and 'the buildings would have become (as is the case with many of the houses in the immediate neighbourhood) seriously dilapidated'. As early as 1827, then, the committee were aware of the problems of the neighbourhood, as well as of the schools, resulting from flooding and bad drainage. Increased manufacturing works and the pressure of population and building made the situation worse.

London, it must be remembered, had no overall administrative body (the London County Council was not created until 1889), and *ad hoc* bodies organised – with difficulty – particular aspects of London life. Lambeth itself, for example, had nine different lighting boards to look after the gas lighting which had been introduced early in the century.[4] The Metropolitan Commissioners of Sewers were responsible for the particular problem with which Lambeth and other parishes were faced.

The campaign in Kennington seems to have begun in 1850. A petition was issued in February by the Rev. Charlton Lane, with a note stating that it was being placed for signature at the boys' school house, in the Kennington Oval, in the charge of Mr Hay, the master. It mentioned that benefit had been derived from those sewers which had previously been laid under the direction of the Commissioners 'in the roads leading from the Kennington Church, through Newington, Walworth, &c.; and, also, from Vauxhall, through Upper and Lower Kennington Lanes, &c', and from some drains laid by the parish surveyors. These drains had been found to be inadequate and imperfect, however, and further sewers were urgently needed, so that householders could lay drains

> thus superseding the formation and use of *cess-pools*, which are not sufficient to relieve buildings from dampness, and their foundations from decay; they are, moreover, found, in many situations, to contaminate the springs and wells of wholesome water, and, therefore, to be injurious to the health of the neighbourhood.

The petition refers to 'the prevalence of an epidemic and fatal disease in and near the neighbourhood', giving rise to the fear that 'causes, similar to those which may have produced, or fostered, diarrhoea and cholera, in the summer of the last year, may again occur'. Without knowing why, the campaigners had in fact fully explained the way in which cholera was primarily spread. It was also pointed out that these facts, and the 'obnoxious effluvia' arising from the overflowing of Effra Creek, which deposited its filth along its route and flooded the houses, affected the social composition of the area: Kennington was close to central London, had easy access by several bridges, and ought to be able to 'afford desirable and convenient residences to persons, whose daily avocations oblige them to go to and from London, or Westminster; but who, in many instances, prefer other localities, less convenient, but with better means of drainage'.

TO THE METROPOLITAN

COMMISSIONERS OF SEWERS.

Kennington, Surrey,
14th February, 1850.

The Representation of the Inhabitant—House-holders of Kennington, and the Vicinity.

RESPECTFULLY SHEWETH,

That the prevalence of an epidemic and fatal disease in and near the Neighbourhood of Kennington, has given much reason to the Inhabitants to fear, that Causes, similar to those which may have produced, or fostered, Diarrhoea and Cholera, in the summer of the last year, may again occur in places, where its effects have recently been experienced.

The under-signed Inhabitants are, therefore, anxious to obtain the early attention of the Commissioners, to the state of the Sewers and Drains in this and the adjoining Neighbourhoods.

The subject of the defective state of Drainage in and about the District of Kennington, has, at different times, been discussed, and it has, on all occasions, been admitted, that the *Health* of the Inhabitants;—the state of the *Buildings*, in reference to their permanence and durability;—the condition of the *Public Roads*, &c. &c.,—demand attention to this important subject.

Great advantages have been derived from the Sewers, which have been formed, under the direction of the Commissioners, in the Roads leading from the Kennington Church, through Newington, Walworth, &c.; and, also, from Vauxhall, through Upper and Lower Kennington Lanes, &c.

Some benefit has also arisen from the Drains which have, in certain places, been laid down by the Parish Surveyors; but these Drains have been found, in some instances, to be *imperfect*, on account of not being sunk to a proper depth, or with a sufficient fall or descent, and not being of a bore, or diameter, sufficiently large to admit of their being efficacious, according to the purposes for which they are intended.

The under-signed Inhabitants are, however, unwilling to address the Commissioners in the language of complaint, but they earnestly request their immediate attention to the formation of *Sewers* in certain Roads, communicating between the Clapham, Kennington, and Vauxhall Roads, into which *Drains* may be formed by the Householders, or Owners, so as effectually to purify and cleanse the Houses on those lines of Road,—thus superseding the formation and use of CESS-POOLS, which are not sufficient to relieve Buildings from dampness, and their Foundations from decay; they are, moreover, found, in many situations, to contaminate the Springs and Wells of wholesome water, and, therefore, to be injurious to the Health of the Neighbourhood.

The sanitary state of the *Buildings*, as well as of the *Occupiers*, requires, therefore, that attention should be given, in every situation, to EFFECTUAL DRAINAGE.

The under-signed Inhabitants are also anxious to draw the particular notice of the Commissioners to the state of the *Effra Creek*, which passes from the Brixton Road, under the Clapham Road; but, being in a very *filthy* condition, it leaves its impurities in its *winding* and *open* passage from the end of Church Street, through South Lambeth, to its junction with the River Thames, near Vauxhall Bridge.

The obnoxious effluvia arising from this unwholesome Creek is attended with another most annoying and destructive inconvenience to the Inhabitants, namely, the occasional overflow of the Neighbourhood by High Tides, passing up the Creek for a considerable distance from the River, keeping its waters in suspense, overflowing the Roads,—inundating the Houses,—and thus seriously damaging the adjoining properties.

The under-signed Inhabitants are induced, respectfully and earnestly, to make this representation to the Commissioners of Sewers, and to entreat their early attention to the state of the Neighbourhood of Kennington; which, *if a proper and efficient mode of Drainage* were established, would, from its contiguity to the Metropolis, and the advantages of easy access, by means of the several Bridges, afford desirable and convenient residence to Persons, whose daily avocations oblige them to go to and from London, or Westminster; but who, in many instances, prefer other localities, less convenient, but with better means of Drainage.

CHARLTON LANE, M.A.,
Incumbent of Kennington in Lambeth.

Note:—This Representation is placed for the signature of the Inhabitants, at the Boys' School House, in the Kennington Oval, in charge of Mr. HAY, the Master.

The campaign for better sewage and drainage continued for at least another three years. An appeal to the Duchy of Cornwall resulted in the Council of the Prince of Wales urging the Com-

missioners of Sewers to take action. The Commissioners informed
the Duchy that as far as the Effra was concerned 'the improvement of this river forms a portion of the proposed works for
the drainage of the South side of the Thames and that the
filling up of the most offensive part of it will be one of the first
works executed'. The Duchy offered a donation of £10 towards
the Kennington Schools' costs in completing their own part
of the proposed drainage. Further letters and reminders to the
Commissioners followed in 1851, bringing the reply that contracts
for the main drainage had been 'some time since entered into by
the Commissioners, but which works have been delayed by the
want of the necessary funds'. An angry petition for improved
drainage in Lambeth as a whole was organised in 1852 (the
place for signing it in Kennington was not the school house,
but the famous Horns Tavern). By 1853 main sewers had
apparently been laid in the roads adjoining the Kennington
Schools, but proper drainage was still needed, the Effra continued to offend, and the problem of cesspools remained a
major one. In appealing for funds to improve the drainage of
the schools, the committee issued the following document, which
gives the clearest possible picture of the schools as a focal point
in the drive for improvements:

KENNINGTON OVAL SCHOOLS:— STATE OF THE DRAINAGE.

KENNINGTON OVAL.
8th July, 1853.

The Committee for superintending the National Schools in
the Kennington Oval are induced to submit to the serious
consideration of the Inhabitants in general the following points
connected with the Cleanliness and Health of the Neighbourhood.

1.—The state of the Buildings and of the Out-offices belonging to
the Schools in the Kennington Oval, has been strongly represented in the Annual Reports of the Schools for several years
past, and is now become such as to render it necessary that
some immediate measures should be taken for the alteration
and improvement of the *Drainage*, and for the removal of
Nuisances which are dangerous to the Health of the Children,
and of Persons who reside in and near that locality.

2.—It is not alone sufficient to point out the advantages which would unquestionably result from the formation of *Drains* of proper dimensions and depth, in connection with the Main Sewers which have been established in the contiguous High Roads; but it is necessary to state that these Drains must, *without further delay*, be at once formed, in order to purify the Buildings, and as far as possible, to prevent disease.

3.—The first object of the Committee of the Schools is to secure a continuance of the Health of the Children, as well as of the Inhabitants of the Neighbourhood in general.

4.—The Privies and Cesspools which exist in many of the houses in Kennington, require cleansing and alteration, so as to render the Houses wholesome and habitable.

5.—In addition to those receptacles of impurity, the inhabitants, particularly those in and near the Kennington Oval, have to bear the sad nuisances arising from the *Effra Creek*, from the filthy state of which the most obnoxious and offensive smells proceed, and seriously endanger the health of the Inhabitants, particularly in the summer season, when the atmospheric humidities and heats prevail to a great extent.

6.—The annoyances are become grievous, and measures should be immediately taken for their removal. It is not enough to complain; it is the remedy, and the removal which must be sought, and at once set about and carried into effect. A house or building, which is infected with a pestiferous and deadly smell, ought not to be inhabited, and no time should be lost in using the means for purifying it.

7.—The Inhabitant Householders owe it to themselves, to their families, and to their neighbours, to use every exertion, and to join in any measures which may be suggested for the removal of these most serious nuisances.

The above remarks are respectfully submitted to the consideration of the Neighbourhood in general, by the Committee of the Kennington Oval Schools.

Signed at request of the Committee,
RICHARD CANNON, *Treasurer.*

NOTE.

With a view to the carrying into effect of the measures which may be advisable for improving the Drainage of the Schools, Donations will be thankfully received, by the Rev. C. Lane, M.A., Kennington Oval; by Mr. Cannon, 5, Kennington Terrace; or by Mr. Hay, Boys' School, Kennington Oval, and applied to the object in view. The cesspools which can be dispensed with, will be filled up, and where they may be still required, they will be removed to a distance from the buildings.

It is obvious that in the absence of proper local government the committee proved in this situation the most suitable local organ through which a campaign could be mounted (and remembering also that there was strong resistance in many parts of the country to making local government services more efficient – and therefore more expensive). At this point in 1853 the interests of the schools and of the neighbourhood were being seen to be identical; this document is about the school-children and the local residents, the school buildings and other buildings, the 'out-offices' of the schools and cesspools in Kennington generally. It is an appeal for funds for the school and an appeal for community action.

In 1853 the General Board of Health had to warn of 'a third visitation of epidemic cholera'. Although it pointed to such dangers as dirt and overcrowding in relation to the disease, the main emphasis of the Board, in accordance with prevalent theory at the time, was on the atmosphere as the disease-carrier: with the risk of cholera 'the purity of the air we breathe' was 'even more essential than the wholesomeness of food and drink'. In 1853 the General Board of Health offered the following set of 'precautions against cholera': to apply urgently for medicine as soon as looseness of the bowels was detected, to refrain from acid fruits and vegetables, to avoid excess of food or long fasting, wet clothes and foggy night air. 'Drunkards', it reminded everyone, 'always suffer most.'[5] The search for explanations went on in Kennington as elsewhere. In 1849 Cannon had written to the Rev. Lane, enclosing a copy of a printed paper with useful hints on the prevention of cholera; Cannon had already had the paper circulated 'particularly among the children of our schools, from which they may learn the advantages to be derived from the judicious use of salt'.

At the same time, however, Cannon explained that 'there can be no doubt, that *impure water* has been one of the causes of the extension of the epidemic disease'. He had been involved, therefore, in re-opening a well 'of very pure spring water, which has existed for many years on Kennington Green, near the Rustic-Seat-Manufactory', but which had become disused. The well had been cleared out and an iron pump erected (and Cannon proposed sending the minister a can of the water to taste). He saw action of this kind as crucial to the fight against disease, and listed what he believed necessary:

Cleanliness must be observed and enforced; – *drainage* must be obtained wherever it can be effected, so as to carry off impurities; – *wells*, and *receptacles* for *wholesome water*, should be formed in several parts of every parish and district; all *collections* of *filth* and *vegetable matter* should be removed or burnt, and not permitted to accumulate for any length of time so as to produce malaria, or an unhealthful atmosphere.

Cannon clearly had the sort of view which impelled Edwin Chadwick to wage his national campaign to defeat disease through environmental engineering. What becomes clear is that the local campaign of 1850–3 was probably based on Cannon's clear view of the health needs of the schoolchildren and the locality, as expressed in his document of 1849 (and his resignation was to follow in 1854).

Although there is no information about the incidence of cholera, when it did come again, among the families of children at the Kennington Schools, another parish school nearby recorded in September 1854 that the master was called in to the committee and 'reported the number of children in attendance had decreased lately from 140, to 108 or 110, and attributed the decrease to the prevalence of cholera – by which many of the children had been kept at home – from illness, or to attend on their sick relatives.' This third cholera outbreak, in 1853–4, was less severe than the previous ones, but in England the main brunt was borne by London, and in London by a small number of areas, including Lambeth and Southwark. The total death roll in England was 20,100, of which 10,738 were in London. At the beginning of September, less than a month before these Lambeth children were being kept at home, the cholera had 'burst out with the force of a volcanic eruption'.[6] It had gone by the end of the year. It is against such a background that one has to see not only the work for sanitation and other urban improvements by such national figures as Edwin Chadwick, but that of local campaigners like Richard Cannon and Charlton Lane; it is a question not only of the General Board of Health, but of the Kennington Schools.

Notes

A bound volume of minutes and other documents, printed and manuscript, 1823–40.

Minute book and correspondence, 1854–6.

Papers relating to drainage, and applications to the Commissioners of Sewers, 1849–54.

Regency Square Schools, minute book, 1852–62.

1 John Tanswell, *The History and Antiquities of Lambeth*, p. 6; *Surrey*, IV, p. 447; A. D. Nash, *Living in Lambeth, 1086–1914*, pp. 64–5.

2 Tanswell, *History and Antiquities*, p. 7.

3 H. H. Montgomery, *The History of Kennington and its Neighbourhood*, pp. 132–5.

4 G. Lawrence Gomme, *London in the Reign of Victoria*, p. 44.

5 General Board of Health, *Notification*, September 20, 1853; *Precautionary Advice to Local Boards with reference to Cholera*, September 15, 1853.

6 Norman Longmate, *King Cholera: the biography of a disease*, pp. 191–5.

Chapter six

The Schools under the Revised Code 1863-70

The Revised Code

From 1863 the school log books kept by the teachers at Kennington fill out aspects of the curriculum, attendance, and routine matters of the schools at work. Although the Revised Code of 1862 introduced basic changes in the financing and inspecting of schools, it is likely that a great deal in the lives of the schools, the children and the teachers remained unaltered from previous decades.

The Revised Code of 1862 introduced the system of payment by results. Under it, separate grants for apparatus, in augmentation of teachers' salaries, and to pupil teachers, came to an end. Maintenance grants for schools were now to be paid to managers of schools in accordance with 'the attendance and proficiency of the scholars, the qualifications of the teachers, and the state of the schools'. Each child over six who attended more than 200 half-days in the year would earn the school an attendance grant plus eight shillings, but would forfeit one-third of this latter grant if he failed to satisfy an individual examination (by an H.M.I. or his assistant) in reading, another third if he failed in writing, and another third if he failed in arithmetic. Children were to be submitted for examination in 'standards', and a strict schedule in each of these three subjects was laid down for each standard. This scheme was an adaptation of one proposed by the Newcastle Commission, which had reported on the state of popular education in 1861; it was designed to control the growing expenditure on elementary education, and to encourage greater attention to the basic subjects. One effect was to alter the role of the inspector and his relationship with the schools, and another was to encourage rote learning and cramming for the inspector's examinations.[1] Although such pressures on the curriculum and teaching methods can be seen in the case of Kennington, they seem to have been resisted more successfully than in most schools. The National and British Societies were in general both opposed to the new scheme.[2]

The impact of the new system on the girls' schools, where Miss Harriett Gibbs was schoolmistress from 1856 to 1871, is clear from her entries about preparations for the inspector's visits. In October 1863 she examined the children who were to be presented to the inspector: 'result frightful especially in arithmetic'. A fortnight later she 'took all the children who were to be presented to the inspector for slate work. Result not very encouraging.' The Rev. C. H. Wyche, who, like the incumbents of St Mark's generally throughout this period, took a keen interest in the school, came in two days later 'and examined the children for the new code. Result most disheartening.' The following day she took 'all the children who were to be examined in all subjects'. Walter Cornell, master of the boys' school probably from 1863 until he left at Christmas 1868, was at the same time also feeling the examination pressures. In March 1863 he abandoned some special arrangement that had previously existed for arithmetic: 'changed organisation for arithmetic, ceasing to have a separate classification for that subject. Intend to try the same classes for reading & writing, on account of new code.' In September of the same year he recorded that 'we are spending much time in arithmetic, in which subject many boys will fail'. In 1864 he introduced 'home lessons', which began to be a regular feature of the boys' school (and probably also of the girls' school). In 1863 the master 'commenced the plan of keeping late scholars half an hour beyond the school hours so as to fulfil the requirements of the new code', and at the end of the decade the boys in general were being kept in to prepare for the inspector's visit – in some cases from 12.30 to 1 p.m. and in others from 4.05 to 5.30 p.m., 'for special work'.

From our point of view here one of the most important features of the new code of regulations was the compulsion on teachers to 'daily make in the log book the briefest entry which will suffice to specify either ordinary progress, or whatever other fact concerning the school or its teachers, such as the dates of withdrawals, commencements of duty, cautions, illness, &c.'. Entries were not to be removed or altered, the inspector would call for the log book at his annual visit, and

summaries of his reports would be entered in it. R. W. Lingen, Secretary to the Committee of Council on Education, explained that the log book procedure should not be difficult to the 'zealous and intelligent teacher': 'The log book is not meant to contain essays ... but to collect items of experience. A teacher who performs this duty simply, regularly, and with discrimination, will find it a powerful help in mastering his profession, as well as an honourable monument of his labours.'[3] It is clear from the tone of many entries at Kennington that the log book was treated in the same way as a diary – as a friend to confide in, providing a simple form of psychotherapy.

The curriculum

The main work in the schoolroom was, of course, scripture lessons and the three staple subjects – reading, writing and arithmetic, though there is little detail about them in the log books. The examination in reading for the most senior children, those in Standard VI, was to be, in the words of the code – 'a short ordinary paragraph in a newspaper, or other modern narrative'.[4] This explains the school master's entry in 1865: 'heard the reading in the 1st. section from the "Times" ' – the only occasion in the 1860s that he mentions this procedure, though it occurs in later decades. There are references in the boys' school at various points in the 1860s also to other subjects, especially when, under the code of 1868 it was possible for schools to earn grant for the teaching of 'specific subjects' other than the three Rs. Grammar, geography and history lessons are all mentioned on one page in 1868 (as is a new list of the Kings of Israel and Judah). Human physiology and object lessons were being taught, and in 1863 the boys were reported to be having 'spelling exercises' which 'appear to be interesting to the children', and the master was 'continuing with the plan of saying tables while the classes are changing their positions'.

Needlework continued to be a dominant feature of the girls' school, and its position was probably no different from what it was in previous decades. In 1863 the mistress mentions that 'in the afternoon a great deal of needlework came from the parsonage – wanted in a hurry. This caused some little disorder

as the work came in late.' One afternoon in 1865 the children
were 'disorderly . . . in consequence of an insufficient supply
of needlework'. Later the same year when the first class had
a lot of needlework to do she 'kept some girls in for half an
hour for being idle'. In 1866, when several lady visitors were
present, she 'let the girls sing while at needlework'. One afternoon
in 1868 there were '18 pocket handkerchiefs sent in wanted
immediately' for the wife of a clergyman. One afternoon the
same year 'the first and second classes had sponge cakes &c
for needlework done for a lady'. By far the most revealing
comment about the status of needlework with the girls themselves is the frank entry in 1867: 'Commenced work this afternoon
with a large attendance in consequence of having told the girls
we were going to have lesson instead of needlework.' That the
church and the parsonage made regular demands on the girls'
skill is also borne out by the occasions when the vicar brought
such items as '40 books to be covered' and 'banners to make
for the treat'. Scripture lessons were frequent, including by
the vicar, both for the children and, out of school hours, for
the pupil teachers. Singing lessons were frequent, and local
ladies regularly helped with these, including by playing the
harmonium.

Attendance

Three entries for the girls' school are reminders of the wider
national problem of literacy. In June 1863 there were 'several
admissions of girls between ten and eleven not able to read or
do any thing creditably'. In April 1866 the mistress admitted
'ten girls several of whom over ten years of age not able to do
anything like lessons; four cannot read'. In June 1869 she
admitted a girl of '12 years of age who had not been to school
before and she did not know her alphabet'. Basic literacy,
measured by the ability of brides and bridegrooms to sign their
name in the parish registers (the criterion commonly used, in
the absence of any other), had been slowly rising from the earlier
decades of the century. In 1840 the literacy rate was probably
about two-thirds for males and a half for females, and by 1870
it was probably about 80 per cent for males and under 75 per
cent for females.[5] Improvements were related to questions of

H

ensuring enough school places and enforcing attendance – both of which were to be preoccupations of the 1870s and the remainder of the century.

It is not possible to relate the attendance figures of the school in any way to the percentage of school attendance in Lambeth. It is only possible to picture the difficulties of ensuring attendance among children already on school books, and in a school which took pains to secure the highest attendance rate possible. The master, we are frequently reminded in his log book, was in the 1860s constantly sending after absentees. The following extracts from the log books of the girls' school, all taken from the period up to the end of 1866, illustrate some of the reasons for a given high level of absence or lateness (though they do not illustrate all the individual, family and other social reasons for absenteeism):

5th January 1863	School opened this morning with very poor attendance in consequence of the wet weather.
24th November 1863	Weather very wet, hardly any children.
8th December 1863	Very wet all day so few in the afternoon that I did not call the names.
11th April 1864	Small attendance in the morning, obliged to give a half holiday in the afternoon in consequence of the demonstration for Garibaldi.
25th May 1864	Small attendance in consequence of the races.
21st November 1864	A good attendance but several children away from sickness and parents being out of occupation.
30th January 1865	Commenced school this morning with a very few girls. Snowing and raining all day.

2nd May 1865	Attendance rather smaller than usual during the week in consequence of the races.
12th July 1865	A small attendance, gave several children leave to go to a Sunday school treat.
28th August 1865	Much excitement in school this afternoon – Children kept in till five o'clock in consequence of the approaching treat)
and therefore 30th August 1865	Small number present, children tired and many late.
9th October 1865	A great many girls late in the afternoon in consequence of a balloon going up from the gas works.
9th November 1865	A small number present in the afternoon – Lord Mayor's day.
11th January 1866	Snowing all day, only 19 girls in the morning and 14 in the afternoon.
29th January 1866	Many girls late this afternoon in consequence of fire in Vauxhall Street.
5th March 1866	A small attendance, many girls away from illness, bad chilblanes and other causes.
16th May 1866	A small attendance all day in consequence of the Epsom races.
21st–25th May 1866	Whitsun week – gave Monday and Tuesday holiday. Assembled the girls on Wednesday only 29 making their appearance gave the rest of the week.
5th November 1866	A small school all day especially in the afternoon – Guy Fawkes.

Similar reasons appear in the boys' log book, and all of these will have been just as operative in previous (and remained so in the following) decades. The races feature widely in other places.

For example, when an H.M.I. inspected a National school at Beccles, Suffolk, in 1845 he found that 'owing to the races, which took place this day, the attendance was thin'.[6] In 1876 the master of Rothley village National school in Leicestershire was recording a 'short attendance' for the latter part of a week in October: 'some children kept at home, others gone to Leicester on account of races'.[7]

Although lateness was often punished by keeping children in after school, in 1869 the mistress records sterner action: 'Many girls locked out'. There is no evidence as to whether the girls saw this as a punishment!

There are remarkably few references in the log books of the two schools to illness as a reason for absence, since the only reasons for absence given are those which affected a large number of children at the same time, and only infectious diseases are therefore mentioned. In November 1867 the mistress 'sent home two children who had been ill with scarlet fever and were not well enough to come to school'. In March 1868 she 'sent home two girls with the mumps'. There is also mention of one girl being refused admission to the school in the same year 'for having a dirty head' – and it is remarkable that there is no further mention of this for the rest of the century. Apart from the day in 1866 which had been 'appointed by the Bishop for fasting and humiliation for the cattle plague', log books display no other interest in sickness in this period. At the Rothley National school in Leicestershire (where reasons for absence were more frequently mentioned, and included everything from haymaking and ploughing to attending the fair and watching the hunt) the sickness question loomed large right from the school's foundation in 1872. Illnesses mentioned in the 1870s included smallpox, scarlet fever, measles, sore throats and whooping cough. An interesting comparison with more urban Kennington is provided by the occasion in 1877 when we find 'children rather late owing to want of correct "time". The church clock is not going.'[8] Kennington children in the 1860s perhaps found it easier to find out the time, but it is unlikely that they had fewer illnesses.

Amusements

The first mention of school treats occurs in August 1865, when the mistress reports that 'the children had a delightful day's pleasure at Richmond Park'. This became a regular school event (at about the same time the previous year girls were given an afternoon's leave 'to go with their parents to the horticultural gardens'). On Ascension Day in 1866 the mistress took the third class to church in the morning and to Westminster Abbey and St James's Park in the afternoon. The treat the following year and for the rest of the decade took place at Hampton Court. On two different days in July 1868 fifty girls and 100 boys were taken to the zoo.

Other occasional respites from routine are also mentioned. On 10 March 1863, when the marriage of the Prince of Wales took place, the children came to school in the morning for their bun and orange and 'then went home for a holiday'. In July 1866 the Rev. Poyntz 'gave the children a half holiday in honour of the Princess Helena's wedding', and another half holiday was reported the following year in honour of Her Majesty's birthday.

Girls in particular were frequently being taken to the Crystal Palace in the 1860s, preparations for church events took children to sing at St Mark's, and in March 1865 the master was even 'putting down names of members of the K.O.S. Cricket Club' (which was to commence practice one evening the following April, and played a match one Saturday against Oval House School). The playground is occasionally mentioned, as in March 1866 when the mistress 'let the children have a game in the playground', and early in 1871 when the extraordinary entry occurs in the boys' log book: 'Boys allowed in the playground for $\frac{1}{2}$ an hour this morning by special request of first class boys'. This was on a Friday, and as the entry for the following Wednesday records a 'half holiday by special request of the boys (Queen opened parliament)', the 1870s would seem to have begun with an exceptional display of school democracy.

Other school-day excitements of the girls (whose teacher was a more faithful diarist than was that of the boys) are also occasionally mentioned. 'Excitement prevailed in consequence of the approaching treat' is a common admission. The girls were reported as 'much excited' in consequence of what the teacher mis-spelt as 'valantines', though the following year she spelled it correctly: 'Much excitement prevailed throughout the school both at the opening in the morning and afternoon many girls bringing their valentines.' There is an intriguing entry in March 1868, when again there was 'much excitement' in the school 'in consequence of a blackman making his appearance to tell of his entertainment'. 'Great excitement' was reported the same year over a girl who had been 'decoyed away from home on her way home from school'. The following day, in her own great excitement the teacher wrote: 'the child found last night last night', and started a subscription to buy the girl 'new clothes, boots, etc.' On Ascension Day, two days later, the school 'returned thanks in Church for God's mercy in restoring her who was lost'. That excitement was common among the girls, or at least that the word was popular with their teacher, was confirmed in March 1869, when the children were reported as 'much excited about the boat race'.

Pupil teachers and monitors

The Revised Code in almost all respects down-graded the teacher – by subordinating his skills to a system which measured them mechanically by their 'results', by reducing his area of initiative and the likelihood of any broadening of the concept of elementary education, and by making his salary dependent on the goodwill of the managers, in the light of the grant earned. It is clear from the Kennington records that in only one respect did the teacher's sense of responsibility in the school increase in this period – his relationship with the pupil teachers, whom he was involved in selecting, supervising and teaching. He was able on occasion to leave the school in charge of the pupil teachers (as in 1863 when he 'took 50 boys to Crystal Palace. Left school under charge of senior pupil teacher'). The mistress regularly recorded, as the regulations required, that pupil teachers had made 'ordinary progress' or had been 'attentive to duty' or some such phrase, and on an occasional Friday had a lapse of spelling: 'The school has made the ordinary progress. The PT's have been obedient, dilligent and punctual during the week.' The pupil teachers, reported the master in 1863, 'are beginning to get an influence over the boys'. In 1868 he 'explained to H. Harman (1st year P.T.) some of his defects in giving scripture lessons', and in 1869 reported: 'Teachers taken early in the morning, instead of in the evening. I found that I was unable to teach them so well after school, being fatigued with the school work during the day.' In November

1869, three days before the arrival of H.M. Inspector, the 'master and the P. teachers swept the walls and nailed defective maps'. The most heartbreaking of his entries occurs in October 1863, when he notes a 'visit from a Winchester candidate for pupil teachership. Lad too small.'

In the girls' school, in May 1864, we find the children disorderly and the 'P.T's not quite so industrious as could be wished', and later in the year we find one of the clergymen visiting the school 'and spoke to the pupil teachers respecting their duties'. The following year the mistress was 'obliged to reprove the P.Ts for bad behaviour in schooltime'. In January 1870, pupil teacher 'E. Pitt gave lesson to the first class in geography which was a great failure', but by March all was well: 'P.T. E. Pitt improved in teaching' (and went on to become assistant mistress). At the same time other pupil teachers were being recorded as giving, in one case 'a very good lesson to the first class', and in another 'a good object lesson to the lower division'. There are occasional references to monitors. In 1868 the boys had a visit from a boy who was 'formerly a monitor' and now worked in an office. In 1863 a monitor in the girls' school 'left in consequence of rudeness' (it is not clear whose). In 1866 there is an enigmatic entry: 'change monitors for next week'. The use of monitors was also an expedient used when the pupil teachers were away, as on the occasion when the pupil teacher had gone off to sit for her Queen's Scholarship and the mistress was 'obliged to get monitors from first class'.

The life of the school

By the beginning of the 1860s the Kennington Schools had also acquired an infant school, under the supervision of the mistress of the girls' school, and a new infant school room was opened in September 1864. Evening classes, as we shall see in the next chapter, were conducted for a short period in both the boys' and girls' schools.

During the 1860s a graduated system of school pence came into existence, at first with $2d.$, $3d.$ and $4d.$, and then, as the master reported in November 1864, 'no child now pays less than 3d.' An undated set of rules in the headmistress's handwriting shows the situation with regard to school pence and other aspects of school life at the beginning of the 1860s:

Kennington Oval Girls School

Rules

I. *Admission*.

Parents are requested to bring their children on Monday morning between 9 and half past.

II. *Payment*.

In junior department 2d. each per week
In the middle classes 3d. ,,   ,,   ,,
In the first class   4d. ,,   ,,   ,,
Where one or more additional children attend from the same family the payment is 3d. each.
Children not admitted under 3 years of age.

III. *Teaching*.

The children are instructed in Holy Scripture, Church Catechism, reading, writing, arithmetic as well as in a general knowledge of grammar, geography, English history and domestic economy. The afternoon of each day is devoted to instruction in *plain* needlework.

IV. *School Hours*.

In the morning from 9.30 a.m. to 12.30 p.m.
,, ,, afternoon ,,   2.0 to 4.0.

Numbers in the infant school were 'considerably reduced' when the fee was raised to 3*d*. per week. School pence now played a somewhat different part in the school's income from what it had done in the years after 1835. The balance sheet for 1866–7, for example, shows the school pence to have been much the largest item of income (nearly £250), the Committee of Council grant next (just over £150), and the endowment, voluntary contributions and collection after a sermon together totalling about the same as the government grant. The success rate of the children submitted at the annual inspection was – combining the figures for the boys and girls – of the order of 90 per cent (in 1865, for instance, it was 87 per cent in reading, 90 per cent in writing and 87 per cent in arithmetic, and 94, 89 and 90 per cent respectively the following year).

The log books indicate that the children were not only rewarded with treats, but also punished – generally by being kept in after school. At the end of one week when the children

had been disorderly the mistress gave a lesson 'to the whole
school on good manners'. On a Monday in 1863 she records:
'not so many girls late today in consequence of having promised
to scramble some lettuces with the early girls'; on Friday of
the same week she writes that she was 'much upset by one of
the mothers coming and swearing most fearfully for nothing
at all'. Bribery and irate parents must have been a feature of
earlier periods also.

The schools were used to receiving a constant stream of
visitors. The clergymen of St Mark's played an integral part
in the life of the schools, as often did their wives and other
ladies of the parish. When the committee met on a weekday
morning (which it usually did in the 1860s), the members often
visited the schools.

Visitors included, of course, the inspectors, and the secretary
of the committee was bound under the Revised Code to enter a
faithful copy of the inspector's reports into the log books; these
reports (usually only a sentence or two at this period) offer a
simple general commentary on the state of the schools. His
report on the boys' school in 1864, for example, reads:

> A very large and important school. Master able and
> intelligent: careful in his work and anxious for the success
> of this school. The religious teaching requires more care and
> attention; at the present time the knowledge of the children
> on the very simplest truths is not satisfactory.

In 1867 he reported that 'the school continues in a thoroughly
satisfactory state. The attainments are above the average both
in elementary and general knowledge. The scripture knowledge
is thoroughly good.' In 1863 the H.M.I. reported that the girls'
school 'appears to be conducted with industry, integrity and
good temper. The upper class appears to have been more
carefully instructed than those below.' In 1866 the school was
'in a satisfactory state. The girls are orderly, quiet in manner
and intelligent.' At the end of 1869 the H.M.I. said of the girls'
school: 'The school maintains its good character. The discipline
and attainments are very creditable. The older girls attend
irregularly. The pupil teachers have passed a very good
examination.' A year later he said of the boys' school: 'The
school is in excellent order, and thoroughly well taught. The
boys have passed a very creditable examination in scripture,

geography, grammar, and mental arithmetic; the elementary knowledge is obviously good throughout. The pupil teachers have been well taught.' Against a background of criticism of the voluntary schools, and demands for a national system of public elementary education, there can be no doubt that the Kennington Schools were consistently achieving standards above the average.

Notes

Log book of the girls' school, 1863–71.

Log book of the boys' school, 1863–80.

1 M. E. Sadler and J. W. Edwards, 'Summary of Statistics', *Special Reports on Educational Subjects*, II, pp. 86–9; *Report of the Committee of Council on Education, 1868–69*, pp. xx–xxv; Mary Sturt, *The Education of the People*, chs 12–13.

2 H. J. Burgess, *Enterprise in Education*, pp. 172–85.

3 The instructions and Lingen's letter were printed in the front of log books published for use in National Schools by the Society.

4 *Report of the Committee of Council, 1868–69*, p. liv.

5 Lawrence Stone, 'Literacy and Education in England 1640–1900', pp. 119–20; Richard D. Altick, *The English Common Reader: a social history of the mass reading public 1800–1900*, p. 171.

6 *Minutes of the Committee of Council on Education, 1845*, I, p. 195.

7 Log book, Rothley National School, Leicestershire, 1872–1907. We are grateful to Mr Richard Luker for this reference.

8 *Ibid.*

Chapter seven

Earnest, reverent and efficient 1870-1900

In the half-century after the foundation of the Kennington Schools, the provision of education for the children of the poor had undergone a considerable expansion. The concept of 'charity' education had been replaced by that of 'elementary' education, but the purpose remained essentially the same – to provide for the children of 'the industrial and poorer classes'.[1] The Elementary Education Act of 1870 was aimed at complementing the system which the National and British Societies had done most to bring into existence, as a specific kind of schooling appropriate to the needs of the 'infant poor'. The 1870 Act left the existing network of voluntary schools intact, and supplemented it with a parallel network of schools run by local School Boards (where the shortage of school places made this necessary). By the 1870s, therefore, a more extensive system of elementary education existed, but its basic social objectives had not changed.

There were, of course, over this half-century important changes at various points in the system. Monitors had been largely replaced by pupil teachers, and teacher training colleges had been created. The elements of a more diversified curriculum had been established, notably in the period before the Revised Code of 1862. State finance had been injected into the provision of education. Other developments in education were also effecting the elementary schools.

At a level below the elementary schools as commonly understood there had been the appearance in the 1840s of the 'ragged schools', designed, as we have seen, to provide food and warmth as much as rudimentary education for the poorest children of the streets, young beggars, criminals, the dirty, the hungry and the half-naked. The schools were created by philanthropists who went out 'into the streets and alleys . . . and invited these miserable outcasts to listen to the language of sympathy and care'.[2] One such ragged school was opened in Lambeth, about half a mile north of the Kennington Schools, in 1851. The fact that it was catering for some of the most pauperised children of the district may possibly have taken a little of the pressure off the Kennington Schools to worry about the very poorest of the children in their catchment area. This ragged school, like many others, was handed over to the London School Board after 1870 (though it continued its independent evening and week-end activities).[3]

At a level above the elementary schools, changes were occurring at the end of the 1860s which were more certainly to affect the work of the Kennington Schools. From the end of the 1860s a small number of scholarships began to become available to boys from elementary schools at some of the endowed grammar schools, as a result of the reorganisation of their charitable foundations through the Endowed Schools Act of 1869. It is generally true, as one historian puts it, that 'secondary school exhibitions were hardly made obtainable in practice by elementary school pupils'[4] – but Kennington became an outstanding exception. This was of profound importance to the boys' school in particular, because its ability to win such scholarships from the beginning of the 1880s obviously affected the school's status in the district. For this, but also for other reasons, elementary education as provided by certain voluntary and Board schools became attractive to parents of a slightly higher social standing than had probably supported schools like Kennington in the past. The Bryce Commission on secondary education, looking back in 1895 at what had been happening with regard to scholarships, described the process as follows:[5]

> in London, Birmingham, and other large towns the public
> elementary school test has long since ceased to differentiate
> the poor from the well-to-do. It is not sufficient, we were
> told, to confine scholarships to public elementary schools,
> as the wage-earning classes have, for various reasons, less
> chance than tradesmen, clerks, and professional men, who
> often now send their children to these schools, sometimes
> with the special object of obtaining scholarships.

This probably exaggerates the extent of 'well-to-do' support for the elementary schools in this period, but it is true that some schools attracted the children of 'tradesmen, clerks and professional men'. Kennington was certainly attracting the two former categories in the early 1870s, but the schools remained primarily for working-class children. By attracting children from upper-working-class and lower-middle-class homes, however, the schools could not be said to be 'instructing the infant poor' in the same sense that they had been doing in previous decades. Instead of distributing clothing and 'rewards', the schools were raising their fees and beginning to win scholarships to grammar schools.

Lambeth, like all of the London suburbs, was in these later decades of the nineteenth century growing and changing rapidly. In the last half of the century the population of Greater London increased from over two and a half to over five and a half million. The rate of increase, however, was not uniform. The percentage increase for each decade, recorded in the following years by the census returns, shows the marked growth in the outer London districts (see Table 9).[6]

Table 9

Year	Percentage	
	London	Outer London
1851	21·2	11·0
1861	18·8	30·5
1871	16·1	50·7
1881	17·4	50·0
1891	10·4	50·1
1901	7·3	45·5
1911	−0·3	33·5

The shifting balance was related to the development of cheap, speculative house building, and to cheap transport. Kennington, for example, was an important omnibus terminus, became in 1861 one end of the first tramway in London (Westminster Bridge was the other end), and a decade later had the first cable and trolley tramway, running south to Brixton Hill.[7] Middle-class and skilled artisan families were involved in the migrations, some coming into London in search of employment, while[8] others may have come from the inner districts of London, many of which had been invaded by the very poor class of people who had lost their homes through the building of railways and the widening of main streets. Throughout the new suburbs people were constantly on the move. 'Southwark is moving to Walworth, Walworth to North Brixton and Stockwell, while the servant keepers of outer South London go to Croydon and other places.' As early as 1848 commerce was invading a residential area of Kennington, for in that year the occupier of a house in Kennington Park Road wrote to the Duchy of Cornwall to complain of the dust caused by his neighbour, whose trade was 'shaker of mats, rugs, carpets, etc.' – 'at breakfast I sometimes get nearly smothered'.

Kennington was near enough to central London to share in the increase of the 'very poor class' of people, and also to develop new areas of middle-class housing. Lambeth as a whole had had a population of 58,000 in 1821; in 1861 it was 162,000 and by 1901 it was 302,000. Whereas the population roughly doubled in Lambeth between the latter two dates, this was nowhere near as great a percentage increase as in districts further from the centre (in the same period Wandsworth, for example, increased from 51,000 to 232,000, and Deptford from 38,000 to 110,000).[9] The Oval, Kennington, and a great deal of Lambeth, was no longer the 'very lonely spot' it had been in the 1820s. The Kennington Schools served a catchment area in which, in the later nineteenth century, there was a range of housing and occupations, from the poorest to the commercial and professional middle classes; it was predominantly working-class but with busy commercial, manufacturing and transport interests. When, in 1888, the vicar wrote to the National Society asking for financial aid to enlarge the schools to provide extra space for eighty infants, he described the district as being 'heavily rated for Board purposes and very poor'.[10]

In 1869 Albert Broomfield was appointed as master of the boys' school; he was to stay for thirty-six years, and to make success in open scholarships an important feature of the school. The first one was obtained by a Kennington boy in 1881 to St Paul's School, and over 160 boys won scholarships to a variety of schools in the next twenty years. Half holidays in honour of boys who won scholarships became a regular occurrence in the schools, an 'honour board' was put up, and announcements of successes in these scholarships were published. Before we consider this and other developments in the life of the schools, however, it is important to note that changes in the social composition of the schools were already in evidence in the early 1870s, and probably before.

In 1860 all the boys, as we have seen, were paying 2d. a week; by 1864 they were paying 3d. or 4d. (in the middle and top classes respectively – the separate infant school contained the 'juniors'). By 1875 the fees were 4d. and 6d., and by the end of the 1880s the fee was 9d. The schools seem to have been strict in applying the fee requirement. In 1878, for example, of a porter's son who had been in the school for more than two years the register records: 'father dead: went to a cheaper school'. In 1887 and 1888 two other children left because they were 'too poor to pay 6d. a week'. Not even such factors as the death, disablement or unemployment of a father now excused the 'infant poor' from having to pay their fee at Kennington.

The increase in fees in 1875 occurred roughly at the same time as schools were being required (under a Committee of Council circular of 1873) to keep admission registers. The boys' register was opened in February 1874 for what was described as 'St Mark's Kennington Oval School, Boys' Department'. For the next two and a half years the head teacher scrupulously completed the column asking for information about the occupation of parents or guardian of new entrants (there is no obvious reason why he stopped doing this in 1876). The first forty children for whom parent's occupation is given (all admitted within the first six months), show the following picture: grainer, wardrobe dealer, blacksmith, printer, coppersmith, traveller (3), carman (2), foreman, lighterman, stationer's collector, house smith, civil engineer, messenger War Office, tramway conductor, butcher (3), poulterer, lithographer, clerk, coach trimmer, butler, cabinet maker, publican, baker, greengrocer, painter, omnibus conductor, wheelwright, bookbinder, hatter, schoolmaster, labourer, bath attendant, detective S. Yard, portmanteau maker. The first ten admissions recorded in 1874 read as shown in Table 10.

The last twenty boys for whom such information is given (between May and July 1876) had parents or guardians who were:

Table 10

No.	Date	Pupil's Name in Full	Date of Birth	If exempt from Religious Instruction	Name and Occupation of Parent or Guardian
1	Feb 16	Rowe Albert	22 July 1864	No	David Rowe Grainer
2	„	Rowe William	9 June 1866	No	— Do —
3	„	Bown William	14 Nov. 1864	No	Elizabeth Bown Wardrobe Dealer
4	„	Smith Dan'l R'd	1 May 1865	No	John George Smith Blacksmith
5	„	Smith Art'r John	22 July 1866	No	George Smith Printer
6	Feb. 23	Sick Alfred	25 Feb. 1866	No	Christian Sick Coppersmith
7	March 2	Streeter Jno Alex'r	6 June 1865	No	Herb't Streeter Traveller
8	Mar. 16	Dutch Chas.	10 Dec. 1861	No	George Dutch Carman
9	Mar. 16	Waters Chas.	13 Feb. 1864	No	Sam'l Waters Foreman
10	„	Cloves Harry Arth'r	1 Feb. 1865	No	W'm Cloves Lighterman

principal warder, foreman, packer, brass finisher, engineer, carman, compositor, small shopkeeper, porter, accountant, tailor, carver, bootmaker, cricket batmaker, clerk, postman, laundress, coachman, dentist (2), coal merchant. Almost all the boys admitted in this period were between the ages of six and twelve, and the column 'last school attended' shows that a high proportion had come from Board schools or private schools. Among the first 100 admissions only two are recorded as having previously attended 'dame schools' (though some of the 'private schools' may have been just that), and only two had been to no school previously (one of these was aged six, and the other aged five – the master's own son). Almost all the children of clerks and skilled artisans (such as stone carvers, engravers and brass finishers) had previously attended private schools, Board schools or other church schools, and were probably, as earlier in the century, moving school as their fathers changed jobs.

The general impression is of a school attended by the children of craftsmen, clerical workers, small shopkeepers and salesmen, and parents whose precise social status is not easy to judge from the description in the register (for example, musicians and boarding housekeepers), as well as a proportion of general manual trades, such as porters, labourers and packers. It is unlikely from what we have seen of the Kennington Schools that their social composition was quite like this before the late 1860s. It is probable that the 1870 Education Act raised the status of public elementary education, and that some skilled artisans and lower-middle-class parents tended to select the 'better' voluntary and Board schools. The reputation of the Kennington Schools would have made it a local focus for parents who wished to do well by their children. In 1875, the National Society conducted an enquiry into the effect on its schools of the working of the 1870 Act, and it asked: 'What decrease in the school subscriptions (if any) do you attribute to the formation of a School Board in the district.' Kennington answered, 'None.'[11]

In the period between the 1870 Education Act and the beginning of the twentieth century there were features of school life at Kennington which, while changing in very many respects, remained similar to what we have seen in previous periods. The fight for regular attendance, for example, went on. In the 1870s and 1880s, girls were sometimes absent in large numbers because of rain, snow, flu and 'parties', and attendance was always very thin after the holidays. When a new headmistress took up her duties in January 1884 average attendance in her first week was eighty-one, and she had to 'send round to the parents to know the reason of the absence of their children from school' (whether in the normal course of events, or as a result of her intervention, the average the following week was 111). On one occasion in December 1881 the girls were sent home as 'only 65 appeared, owing to the excessive darkness and bad weather'. In the boys' school, large-scale absences are recorded in the 1880s and 1890s at times of other school fêtes, the boat race, bad weather and good weather. In January 1881, for example, snow falls were so heavy that the school was 'practically closed – no regular lessons were given or registers marked. The school however was opened for those scholars who lived near or who wished to come.' In May 1886, on the other hand, the master recorded that 'the parents often give their children a holiday without a reasonable excuse (such as on a fine day allowing them to go out to enjoy the weather) it seems impossible to get them to alter this habit'. Even in 1902 Mr Broomfield was reporting irritably that 'Dan Leno

I

at the Oval Cricket Ground played sad havoc with the attendance on Wednesday'. There is no doubt that the pressures of the parliamentary acts which made education compulsory and slowly raised the age of exemption from full-time schooling were making headway in achieving more regular attendance in London during the last two decades of the century. From the outset the London School Board established a network of school 'visitors' to try to secure regular attendance (not only in Board schools).[12] The first entry in the Kennington log books which indicates the connection occurs in January 1873, when the headmistress writes: 'School board visitor called on Tuesday to know if there were any absentees to be looked after' – and the school Board visitor is mentioned regularly from then onwards.

Numbers continued to fluctuate. In the girls' school in 1873 weekly averages would vary between under 100 and more than 200. In June of that year the mistress reports – 'attendance gradually improving both in number and regularity. Average for week 190.4' (in a snowy week in February it had been 99, followed by a week at 159, one at 160 and one at 175). On one occasion in May 1888 when there were 150 girls present 'they were allowed ten minutes play as it was the highest number present for a long time'. The average attendance in the girls' school in May of that year was, in fact, 126, out of a total of 164 on the books. This figure (77 per cent) compares with an average attendance in the same month of 249 out of 310 in the boys' school (80 per cent). The boys' school normally had about 300 on the books from the early 1880s, and the girls' total fluctuated between well under 150 and – on a small number of occasions – over 200.

Both the boys' and girls' schools remained firmly geared to the pressures of the inspector's examination, which dictated the schools' grant under the Codes. The Code itself underwent modifications throughout this period. Through the introduction of 'specific subjects' from 1868 and 'class subjects' from 1875 it became possible for schools to earn grant for submitting individual older pupils (in the former case) or whole classes in subjects other than the three Rs, and thus slightly to diversify the curriculum. The following results of the inspectors' visit to the boys' school in 1883 show, among other things, the specific and class subjects in that year (physiology also features as a specific subject in other years for boys, as does domestic economy for the girls):

Report Rec'd 14 Dec. 1883

Abstract of results

Average attendance on which the grant is payable – 243

Fixed grant	4	6
Merit	2	0
Singing from note	1	0
94 per cent @ 1d. %	7	10
Class subjects		
English 2/–		
Geography 2/–	4	0
	19s.	4d.

Specific subjects

Algebra 27
Euclid 5 $= 32 @ 4/-$

Present for examination	235
Absent without excuse	0
	235

Passed in reading	231
,, ,, writing	219
,, ,, arith'c	212
	662

Total grant: 243 @ 19/4 =	£234.18.0
32 @ 4/-	6. 8.0
	£241. 6.0
Honour cert. Children's fees	1. 1.6

Payment on the results of the examination of individual children was more or less ended in 1890, and definitively in 1898. The Kennington log books began to record more simply, as in the girls' school in 1890:

Schedule of grant

On average attendance	£131. 4. 0.
,, specific subject	7.10. 0.
Per head, 20/6	£138.14. 0.

School life contained the same sort of elements that we have seen earlier, including occasional visits, treats and holidays. School holidays in this period were generally two weeks at Christmas, ten to fourteen days at Easter, a day or two at Whitsun, and – from the late 1880s – four weeks in the summer. In 1879 the school songs for the girls were listed as:

1. Wandering minstrels
2. How I love to see thee
3. I love the merry spring time
4. Lo the sun is o'er the hill-top
5. Ripe strawberries
6. See how merrily the skaters go
7. May is here
8. Music

School songs were to remain the strongest bastion of ruralism in urban England. In June 1900 the headmistress reported that 'a piano has been obtained for the school, the result of donations and a collection amongst the scholars'.

Some important changes in the range of school activities can be seen in the last two decades of the century. In June 1880, for example, the boys' school was taking advantage of the opening of the privately-owned Crown swimming baths (municipal baths were not created until the 1890s). In October of 1880 swimming matches had to be postponed 'on account of the breakdown of the warm water apparatus at the Baths', but one day the following week an 'examination for certificates and prizes (swimming) took place at the Crown Baths at half past 10', with several clergymen present. Future log book entries for the 1880s were to report passes for certificates, winners of races, championships, and games of water polo. Activities in the girls' school in 1900 included writing essays on cruelty to animals (as these were posted they were probably in connection with some competition), electing a May Queen, visiting (the first class only), the Victoria and Albert Museum, having a day's holiday on Ascension Day and on the following day also to celebrate the relief of Mafeking, and an afternoon's holiday 'to witness arrival of Princess Henry of Battenberg to lay foundation stone of Belgrave Hospital' (just near the Oval).

So far as can be judged the girls do not seem to have been subjected to severe punishments in this period. In 1880 the headmistress 'had occasion to give a punishment to Charlotte Bowden for impertinence her mother refused to allow her to do it (a task of 300 lines) consequently she is no longer one of the pupils of the Oval School'. It is clear from entries in 1882 that noise and disorder in classes under assistants resulted in the headmistress reprimanding the assistants, not the children. Mr Broomfield in the boys' school, however, had a sterner view of punishment than his predecessors seem to have had. In 1883 two boys who had been warned for playing truant 'were placed across the form and received 6 strokes each'. One of them received the same punishment the following week for the same offence. Later the same year a boy 'received 4 strokes on the hand for continued disobedience'. These are the first cases of corporal punishment recorded in the school's log books (though this does not mean that it had never occurred before). The master also kept boys in late as a punishment, and one entry in 1888 reads as follows:

Bevis – stand'd iv – was dismissed for gross swearing. This was not the first offence by many. He is unfortunately a boy of very depraved mind – though he possesses good ordinary ability for lessons.

Climpson – stand'd iv – A new boy who has been imprisoned for robbery, was also requested not to come to school again. He had been doing very badly during the short time that he had been in the school.

Alongside the obvious disciplinarian efficiency of Mr Broomfield there is clear indication of an understanding of delicate and backward children. In March 1881, for instance, there are three separate entries:

> *Searle*, who is of delicate health, though willing to work, resumed work in standard ii; – his proper standard. It would be a case of overpressure to try to pass him 2 standards this year.
>
> *Geo. Baker* standard i withdrawn last year is still quite an imbecile. Instructed Mr. Heath not to expect this boy to be able to learn anything.
>
> *Donald Davies* (stand'd iv) who has been suffering from diseased eyes, has been excused all work when he feels unfit to do any. He will be withdrawn at the end of the year, should he still continue to suffer.

The master continued to record children who were not submitted for examination or were not promoted to a higher standard because they were, for instance, 'naturally dull and backward', suffered from ill health, or were 'very delicate'. Broomfield's attitude comes out most clearly in an entry describing a new boy as 'old – but seems unable to do his work. Intellectually weak. The Asst. Master has been instructed not to press him.'

Separate class teaching was now taking place, in the case of the boys probably from about 1865, when the Committee of Council made a grant of £59.10s. perhaps towards some additions. In 1888 the dimensions of the school rooms were recorded as shown in Table 11.[13]

Table 11

	length	breadth	height
Boys	56 ft	22½ ft	14 ft
Girls	,,	,,	,,
Infants	28	,,	,,
Classroom boys	44	,,	,,

The development towards separate classrooms was related to the development of the concept of 'assistant teachers', as deputies to the head teacher, and able to take full responsibility for classes. In the country as a whole at the time of the 1870 Education Act there were only just over 1,000 of such assistant teachers; by 1895 there were 28,000.[14] At Kennington there is mention of a salary of £12.10s. for an 'assistant master' in the boys' school in 1868. Twenty years later at the time of the annual inspection the log book records the staff of the boys' school as being:

Head Teacher
    Albert Broomfield: Certificated Teacher
Assistant Teachers:

George W. Whiting	Certificated Teacher
Alfred Heath	Do
George Wilson	Ex. P.T.
Samuel Lucas	Ex. P.T.
Robert Hall	Ex. P.T.

As early as July 1862 the mistress of the girls' school, Harriet Gibbs, was reported by the committee to have two monitors: 'her wish is to have an assistant teacher in place of 2 monitors'. By 1891 the girls' school had three assistant teachers. In 1885 one of the 'assistant masters' (the words 'master' and 'teacher' were used quite indiscriminately in the log book) left under a cloud:

> His conduct was open to grave suspicion previously; and on this day he caused a disturbance to [be] made outside the school by a man to whom he was indebted. He was already under notice to leave the service of the managers.

Not until after the turn of the century do we find mention of assistant mistresses in the boys' schools (in 1905 Mr Broomfield was to find them 'personally all that could be desired', but unable to cope with the work; his successor manoeuvred one of them into resigning the same year). The growth in the number of assistant teachers in schools, the experience of the pupil teacher system, the search for certification – all these are part of the story of the growing sense of professional identity among elementary school teachers, symbolised by the creation of the National Union of Elementary Teachers in 1870 (it dropped the word 'Elementary' from its title in 1889).[15]

The main change at Kennington was undoubtedly in terms of academic emphasis and efficiency, notably in the boys' school, as measured by the inspector each year, performance in Science and Art Department examinations, and success in open scholarships to grammar schools and other institutions. We have already seen this process taking place, in connection with the social status and composition of the schools. As part of a picture of the schools at work these developments are crucial, and they mark a period when Kennington was less typical of National schools generally than at any other time in its history.

From 1874 the log books table the results obtained in the drawing examinations conducted by the Science and Art Department (in that year out of 102 presented in drawing, 49 received a Pass and 12 an Excellent). In 1877 the school was given a half holiday 'on account of the good results of the drawing examination'. In 1885 the results were as shown in Table 12.

Table 12

	Excellent	Certificates	Totals
1st grade drawing to scale	24	42	66
„ „ freehand	8	41	49
„ „ geometry	7	4	11
„ „ model	4	4	8
	43	91	134

Also marked fair 102
Grant for year £16.2.0

A 'science school' was also conducted by Mr Broomfield on two evenings a week, and students were submitted for the Science and Art Department examinations in animal physiology and mathematics. On the first evening it opened in September 1879 thirty-six students were enrolled, varying in age between ten and seventeen, seven of the students being pupil teachers.

Attempts had been made, even in the early 1860s, to conduct evening schools on the premises. Miss Gibbs had asked for an assistant teacher in 1862, because she had had '4 or 5 applicants indicating a great wish for a school in which girls above 12 who have left school may continue to be instructed in connection with the school'; with an assistant she proposed 'to superintend and conduct the evening school'. Such classes were started, in fact, in 1864, but with an attendance of no more than five, and the classes seem to have been quickly discontinued. Similar classes for boys were started at the same time, with greater success, but were ended in February 1865 when the master reported that 'the evening classes were given up as I found their continuance inconsistent with a due discharge of duties in the day school'. Broomfield, however, was made of sterner stuff.

From 1881 boys began to win scholarships to a number of schools, including Archbishop Tenison's, Haberdashers', Bancroft's, Dame Anne Bacon's, St Olave's, Stationers', St Dunstan's, Christ's Hospital and Whitechapel. At the beginning these were normally in ones or twos, but at some places groups of Kennington boys began to carry off the scholarships (and on at least one occasion a girl was also successful). The highest number was twenty-three in 1890. The school publicised these successes, and often the running total of scholarships won. When two boys won scholarships to St Olave's Grammar School, Southwark, the headmaster recorded, in March 1888, that the total number of such scholarships gained by boys from the Kennington school was thirty-nine. The leaflet which the headmaster had printed read:

Kennington Oval Boys' School.

ST. OLAVE'S GRAMMAR SCHOOL ENTRANCE SCHOLARSHIPS.

THE following particulars are sent for the information of the Parents:—

The above Scholarships are of the Annual Value of £11 11s. 0d., tenable for two years, but renewable on the recommendations of the Head Master of St. Olave's School.

The Examinations are held about February of each year.

On 28th February, 1888, an Examination was held in connection with the above Scholarships.

GODDARD, EDWIN, Aged 11,

FELCE, PERCY, „ 12,

of this School, were two of the successful Candidates.

Every endeavour is made by the Staff to ensure success at these Examinations, *but the competition is very keen,* and it is impossible for irregular boys to be successful.

The usual holiday in honour of the event will be given some Friday afternoon after the Easter Holidays.

ALBERT BROOMFIELD,
Head Master.

29th March, 1888.

Two years later, announcing further successes and the usual half-day holiday, the headmaster indicated a staggeringly high total of awards already won:

Kennington Oval Boys School.

OPEN EXHIBITIONS AT STATIONERS' SCHOOL.

The Value of these Exhibitions is £4 a year, viz., half the fees of the School.

On 6th September, 1890, an Examination was held in connection with the above Exhibitions.

Six were gained by boys of the Oval School. Their names in order of merit are—

ROBERTSON, ALFRED ERNEST, Aged		12.
CHILDS, WILLIAM CECIL,	,,	12.
PAPWORTH, HARRY,	,,	11.
KENNY, JOHN M. P.,	,,	12.
COOPER, VICTOR,	,,	12.
DICKINS, CHARLES CYRIL,	,,	11.

Eighty Scholarships have now been gained by boys of this School since 1881.

There will be a half-holiday next Friday in honour of these successes.

ALBERT BROOMFIELD,
Head Master.

September, 1890.

Broomfield was obviously on the look-out for scholarships for which to enter his boys. He entered in the log book in 1892:

'Answers were received from the Head Master of Dulwich (Lower School), Mercer's, & Haberdashers' School (Hatcham) stating that no open scholarships were available for competition by boys of this school . . . '. At the beginning a half holiday was given every time a boy won a scholarship, but the backlog of half-days grew, and the principle of a half-day for every six successes was introduced.

There can be no doubt that these results were exceptional. The number of such scholarships by which elementary school children could climb the 'ladder' to secondary education was severely restricted. St Olave's Grammar School, Southwark, was one of the schools at which Kennington boys won entrance scholarships, for example in 1888 when two boys, Edwin Goddard (aged 11) and Percy Felce (aged 12) won them. The first such scholarship had been granted by St Olave's in 1865 'to enable a poor orphan of remarkable ability to complete his education,' but this was described in 1889 as having developed into a number of 'entrance, promotion, and intermediate scholarships, which enable boys from our own and the neighbouring elementary schools to rise gradually till they attain our exhibitions at the university, etc.'.[16] The number of such scholarships was small and, as Broomfield rightly indicated on the printed announcement of the successes, 'competition is very keen'. The record of Broomfield and Kennington boys in winning such scholarships must have been outstanding by comparison with other elementary schools. The proportion of boys entering Kennington who ended by winning a scholarship was, of course, tiny, but Broomfield's objectives and success rate must have influenced standards and objectives throughout the boys' school in particular, but probably in the girls' school also. Broomfield's log book for 1888 indicates some of the higher level work going on:

Feb 6 to Feb 10

. . . The Head Master was engaged (when possible) this week in special preparation of Stand^d vii boys under 13 for St Olave's Grammar School Entrance Scholarships . . .

The arrangements for Euclid French & Drawing are not satisfactory; with limited room it is difficult to make them so . . .

It was common for Broomfield to teach a group of the top boys in his office.

In 1867, two years before Albert Broomfield was appointed to the Kennington boys' school, Matthew Arnold had lamented in one of his annual reports as an H.M.I. that one of the effects of the Revised Code and payment by results had been that 'the better instructed top class, composed of children who stayed long enough to profit by careful teaching, who received this teaching, and who became, when they left school, a little nucleus of instruction and intelligence in their locality, has for the most part disappeared'.[17] Although this was probably always less true of Kennington than of other National schools, it was certainly far from being true of the school by the beginning of the 1880s. The general comments about the boys' school made during the 1880s and 1890s by the H.M.I.s indicate that the work of the whole school was, in fact, governed by the headmaster's obvious search for a high level of attainment. In 1882 the H.M.I. said that 'the evenness and accuracy of the elementary subjects in the several standards, and the instruction in class and specific subjects in the upper classes deserves the very highest praise'. Whatever criticisms the inspectors had, they were rarely of the elementary work. The report for 1884 began:

> The school is in good discipline and has passed an excellent examination on the whole. *The elementary subjects* excepting *reading* in the second standard have been very successfully taught, *spelling* throughout and *arithmetic* in the first and sixth standards deserving special praise. *Geography and mapping* are superior, the answers being unusually accurate and intelligent.

Four years later the H.M.I. began his report with: 'The school is in the highest state of efficiency and is admirably conducted by Mr Broomfield.' Perhaps the clearest statement of the general condition of the school in this period is contained in the 'report of religious instruction' after the annual visit of the diocesan inspector in 1887. His report began with 'general remarks':

> This is a thoroughly good school. Not only is the syllabus work carefully prepared but the standard of religious

instruction is a high one and the moral training of the boys
is of the best kind being both practical and illustrative.
This is well seen in the earnest reverent tone of the whole
school.

In the girls' school there were changes of headmistress during
this period, and the academic incentives will not have been the
same as in the boys' school, but the majority of reports on the
school in these decades were also favourable, as in the case of
the H.M.I.'s report in November 1888:

> *Girls' School*. The school is in excellent discipline, & has
> passed a very good examination on the whole. The
> elementary subjects have been uniformly well taught
> throughout. The Grammar has improved, & in the three
> lower Standards is very good. The Recitation merits much
> commendation. In Needlework the specimens deserve the
> highest praise, & the exercises, excepting button-holes in
> the fourth Standard, are very creditable. The papers on
> Domestic Economy are satisfactory. The Singing & Drill
> are good; and the Home Lesson Books have been very
> neatly kept.

In competition with the rate-supported Board schools many
of the voluntary schools (and the National Society itself) were
encountering financial difficulties by the late nineteenth century,
and they were often less able to evolve higher-level work than
some of the Board schools. School boards in certain areas,
especially in the North of England, were encouraging the
development in the last quarter of the nineteenth century of
'higher grade' schools, which collected together the senior
children and offered them generally a higher education which
was scientific and vocational in character. Board schools were
widely developing 'ex-standard' or 'higher top' classes, and this
was true of London where Conservative opposition on the
School Board held back the development of higher grade schools
until the late 1890s.[18] Although some voluntary schools were
developing along similar lines, few of them can have been as
successful as St Mark's, Kennington, in maintaining a high
level of efficiency and attainment. Part of the motivation
behind the 1902 Education Act was to provide more financial

help for the voluntary schools. St Mark's entered the twentieth century more successfully than most. It was 'in the highest state of efficiency' and had an 'earnest reverent tone'. This was no doubt true of the school for the most part from its foundation, but the phrases meant something different at the end of the century from what they would have meant in 1824. From the 1860s St Mark's can be seen in some respects to have altered its educational and social objectives. The work of instructing 'the infant poor' in the earlier sense was now being carried on elsewhere.

Notes

Log books of the boys' school, 1863–80, 1880–95, 1895–1908.

Log books of the girls' school, 1863–71, 1872–99, 1899–1913.

Master's and Mistress' Report Book, 1863–95.

Admission register, St Mark's Kennington Oval School, Boys' Department, 1874–82.

General Registers of the Science School, Kennington Oval School, 1879–88, 1888–91.

Account book, 1854–1901.

1 This kind of phrase was still common and is taken here from the sub-title of a book published in 1871 by George C. T. Bartley, *The Schools for the People, containing the history, development, and present working of each description of English school for the industrial and poorer classes.*

2 'The London Ragged Schools', abridged from the *Quarterly Review*, Ragged School Union, *Occasional Paper No. III.*

3 Survey of London, xxiii, *South Bank and Vauxhall*, pt i, pp. 142–3; A. D. Nash, *Living in Lambeth 1086–1914*, p. 61.

4 R. L. Archer, *Secondary Education in the Nineteenth Century* (1966 edn), p. 171.

5 Schools Enquiry Commission, *Report*, I, pp. 168–9.

6 *Royal Commission* on the Distribution of the Industrial Population, *Minutes of Evidence*, p. 399.

7 Nash, *Living in Lambeth 1086–1914*, p. 65.

8 Survey of London, xxvi, *The Parish of St. Mary Lambeth*, pt ii, pp. 11–12.

9 Nikolaus Pevsner, *London*, p. 37.

10 National Society, St Mark's file.

11 *Ibid.* The enquiry was dated 4 January 1875.

12 For a discussion of these questions as they affected London generally in this period see David Rubinstein, *School Attendance in London, 1870–1904: a social history.*

13 National Society, St Mark's file.

14 M. E. Sadler and J. W. Edwards, 'Public Elementary Education in England and Wales, 1870–1895', *Special Reports on Educational Subjects 1896–7*, p. 46.

15 The N.U.E.T. formed local associations, of which the Lambeth Teachers' Association was one. For an interesting glimpse of the

Lambeth body, and its relations with the H.M.I. for the district in the 1880s, see G. A. Christian, *English Education from Within*, pp. 46–7.

16 The Rev. Andrew Johnson, Head Master of St Olave's, quoted in R. C. Carrington, *Two Schools: a* *history of the St. Olave's and St. Saviour's Grammar School Foundation*, p. 212.

17 Francis Sandford (ed.), *Reports on Elementary Schools 1852–1882 by Matthew Arnold*, p. 120.

18 Rubinstein, *School Attendance in London*, pp. 32–3.

Chapter eight

Non-provided, voluntary aided, primary: the twentieth century

1900–18

By the time education in London was reorganised in 1903, St Mark's (N.) School Kennington-Oval, or Kennington Oval School (the London County Council used both names), was in a physical condition which was inadequate to the educational demands being made upon it. In the late 1890s, it is true, £571 had been spent on repaving the girls' playground, re-laying the drains and building a new boys' cloakroom, the funds for this purpose coming from the following sources:[1]

Subscriptions and collections	£337
Church Schools Union	50
Surplus balance school account	129
Ecclesiastical commissioners	30
National Society	25
	£571

St Mark's, like other voluntary schools, had been overtaken, however, by the better appointed, larger Board schools, with their architecture and teaching based on the concept of separate classrooms. By comparison with the urban Board schools most voluntary schools were now old-fashioned, or in a poor state, and unable to make many of the new departures which, as we shall see, elementary schools were beginning to consider. The position of the voluntary schools was particularly serious in the towns, where they were in direct competition with the Board schools. In 1901 the Bishop of Rochester wrote to the Conservative Prime Minister, Lord Salisbury, about the Church schools:[2]

If the schools are not in some way relieved many will go within the year – enough to greatly weaken the cause, and, by creating the impression that 'the game is up', to bring down others in increasing numbers and at an accelerating rate. I am speaking of what I know.

It was partly with the intention of providing such relief that the 1902 Education Act was formulated. This act, followed in 1903 by a separate one concerned with London, did away with the School Boards and made county and county borough councils responsible – with some exceptions – for both elementary and secondary education. The councils were to give financial support to both their own ('provided') and voluntary ('non-provided') schools.

The 'body of managers' of a non-provided schools such as St Mark's were to retain control of the school, with the voluntary body nominating four of the six managers. Non-provided schools were to 'carry out any directions of the local education authority as to the secular instruction to be given in the school'. They were to follow the instructions of the local authority regarding the number and qualifications of staff, accept inspection by the local authority and submit proposed appointments to the local authority for its consent. The financial return to the voluntary schools for this arrangement was contained in the following clause of the 1902 Education Act:[3]

> The managers of the school shall provide the schoolhouse free of any charge, except for the teacher's dwelling-house (if any), to the local education authority for use as a public elementary school, and shall, out of funds provided by them, keep the schoolhouse in good repair, and make such alterations and improvements in the buildings as may be reasonably required by the local education authority; provided that such damage as the local authority consider to be due to fair wear and tear in the use of any room in the schoolhouse for the purpose of a public elementary school shall be made good by the local education authority.

The voluntary body would, therefore, as in the case of St Mark's, provide and maintain the buildings, except for 'fair wear and tear'; it would make its own decisions about religious education, and ensure a standard of elementary education acceptable to the local authority; the authority would in return pay, as in their own schools, for the provision of education (including

K

salaries, and 'fair wear and tear'). This pact, strongly contested by the nonconformists, was the means of putting the Church schools on a sounder financial basis. It made expansion of the voluntary system difficult by not providing grants for the building of new schools, but it rescued and perpetuated the dual system in the public elementary schools.

As was pointed out by the influential Fabian Society at the time of the passing of the 1903 London Education Act, the fact that 'the foundation managers are required by law to provide the structure free of expense, in good condition, and to keep it so', meant substantial new obligations for voluntary schools wishing to remain open as public elementary schools:[4]

> It will be necessary for the Council to have a survey of all the non-provided schools by a competent staff or surveyors . . . The same standard of sanitation and structural efficiency must be enforced in one set of public elementary schools as in the other. We must not let the children's health or comfort suffer, any more than their education, on account of the school buildings being provided by a religious body.

The London County Council did, in fact, undertake a survey and inspection of all non-provided schools. The process of adapting St Mark's to the twentieth century began in earnest in 1905.

In that year the chief inspector reported to the L.C.C. that, in general:[5]

> During the inspection of non-provided schools it has become increasingly apparent that one of the most serious factors in the lack of efficient teaching in the majority of schools is the want of a sufficient number of children in the various departments to admit of proper grading without an unduly extravagant staff. The school accommodation, moreover, does not provide for enough classrooms to make division into a sufficient number of classes practicable, even if it were otherwise possible. To remedy this serious defect, the re-organisation of the school, or portions of the school, has been proposed in a large number of cases.

In the case of Kennington, surveyed in 1904 and reported on

the following year, the architect's report was extremely critical. The lighting, heating and cloakrooms were poor, and there was a lack of workshops, laboratories and other specialised rooms. The premises would be suitable for an elementary school 'if restored'. A 'considerable amount' would need to be spent; the site was suitable, but the buildings were entirely unsatis- ' factory. The managers were instructed by the L.C.C. to carry out a list of twenty-two important alterations and improvements by December 1906, and to reduce the number of children in the school. The target of the managers and the old School Board had been 506, the actual average number on the books in 1904 had been 458, and this was now to be reduced to 442. It was recommended that the separate girls' and infant departments be combined under a single headteacher, and that a teachers' room be provided for this department. In December 1905 the committee replied to the L.C.C. that they had in hand a scheme for raising the necessary money, and in the meantime they confirmed that they were 'prepared to carry out all reasonable requirements'. The L.C.C. architects expressed the view in 1904 that 'no re-arrangement will make the existing buildings entirely satisfactory and it is not worth the expenditure that will be required to put the premises in proper order'. In May 1905 the L.C.C. declared, 'in view of the extensive alterations necessary to the premises that they should be rebuilt'.[6]

It was the scheme for improvements, however, not rebuilding, that went ahead. This took longer than expected, and not until 1907 were the structural alterations, repairs, new fittings, drainage, and other improvements approved and carried out. The Board of Education (created in 1900) had been asked to approve the capitalisation of part of the Forest Endowment to cover a proportion of the expense. The £1,200 raised in this way formed the main part of the total of £1,780 collected in 'subscriptions and collections'; the Diocesan Local Board contributed £120, and the National Society gave £200.[7] The school closed for three months on 1 November 1907, to allow the work to be completed, and the treasurer reported to the committee the following October that 'the improvements were recognised by the Board of Education as satisfactory'. The girls' and infant departments were combined under a single headmistress, and staffroom accommodation was improved. By spending something over £2,000 the school had survived into an age when public elementary schools were required to be certified as 'efficient'.

Numbers were to become a problem. In the boys' school the original maximum of 204 was lowered to 194, and though the number on roll was generally about this figure at first, it began to be difficult to maintain it. During the First World War plans to increase the accommodation for the boys were turned down by the L.C.C. on the grounds of insufficient numbers; the managers recorded in June 1915 that 'unless the present attendance in the boys' school increased', the Council 'would not maintain the additional class-room'. Numbers in the combined girls' and infant department were easier to sustain (and in March 1916 the headmistress recorded in her log book: 'children under five ceased to be admitted').

The period from the beginning of the twentieth century up to the end of the First World War was one, therefore, in which the school was in a much fuller sense part of a national (not just a National) system – and the unit of planning and concern for physical and educational standards was, in the case with which we are concerned, London. The new local authorities that had been created by the Local Government Act of 1888, and had acquired the extended educational powers of 1902 and 1903, had the whole range of local services to worry about. It it clear from the case of Kennington, however, that the L.C.C. was determined that the public elementary schools should match up to the promise of the act which had given it responsibility for them. Although there was protest from nonconformist, liberal and socialist bodies against public financial support for denominational education, the country at large – and certainly London – soon settled down to the reality of an elementary school system which was in one sense divided (or 'dual') and in another sense to a great extent unified.

During this period the benefits of other late-nineteenth-century developments began to be felt in the elementary schools: in the last quarter of the nineteenth century Britain had finally committed itself to compulsory education, had accepted a measure of collective responsibility for welfare, and had begun to broaden the conception both of the elementary school curriculum and of the abilities and individuality of the children.

Education had been made compulsory by law in England and Wales in 1880, and school attendance and the percentage of literacy had improved in the last decades of the century. In the early part of the twentieth century average attendance at Kennington rarely dropped below 90 per cent in any quarter. Two typical years for the boys' schools, for example, are 1909 and 1910, when the average annual attendance was 92·3 and 91·7 per cent respectively. Illness and bad weather remained major factors affecting attendance. The boys' school in 1911 and 1912 recorded boys being absent with scarlet fever, one with a 'slight attack of scabies', and one who was excluded for being verminous (and whose mother stated it to be 'skin disease, hereditary'); the log book also recorded the 'death of B. Gorden, scholar, who had been absent for nine months suffering from ringworm'. The headmistress frequently referred to reasons for 'variations in attendance', including such things as epidemics of measles, influenza or scarlet fever; she mentioned poor attendance 'after an all-night thunderstorm' in 1916, and in foggy or snowy weather.

The beginning of the twentieth century had seen an increasing sense of public responsibility for social problems which in the nineteenth century had been tackled at best by acts of charity. Welfare was an outstanding example. Reasons included pressures from political organisations and educationists (Margaret McMillan's work for school health services span both, since she was a member of the Independent Labour Party and a pioneer of child welfare services). They also included a heightened awareness of the extent and causes of poverty, as revealed especially in Charles Booth's study of *The Life and Labour of the People of London,* carried out mainly in the 1890s, and a realisation of the low level of health among the poorer sections of the community, revealed by would-be recruits during the Boer War. The result, under the 1906 Liberal government, was the first school meals act (enabling local authorities to spend rates for this purpose) in 1906, and an act in 1907 which inaugurated the school medical service; other acts, between 1908 and 1911, aimed to protect children, and introduced old age pensions, and unemployment and health insurance. This sharpened interest in health and welfare is reflected in the Kennington log books and committee minutes. The school nurse, for example, now visited the school ('and examined heads'). At several meetings in 1911 the managers discussed the case of a girl whose father objected to her being examined by the school nurse. The L.C.C. told the managers that as the parent consistently refused to submit her for inspection, 'the said child should be excluded from attendance'. The matter was resolved when the father wrote to the L.C.C. undertaking to submit a certificate from his own doctor with regard to the condition of his child's hair whenever required 'and that on this understanding the child may be allowed to resume school'.

In addition to the creation of national services of this kind, other activities developed in relation to the health of poor children. London, for example, in 1908–9 created a network of 'school care committees', consisting of voluntary workers who looked into cases of children requiring free meals, were present at medical inspections and acted as liaison with the homes of children shown to have health or other problems. The Secretary of the Children's Care Committee was reported in the boys' log book as having visited the school in January 1910, to make 'enquiries concerning the Children's (School) Care Committee for this school'. She was informed that such a committee 'did not exist at this school', but in March the headmaster reports a first meeting of a Care Committee which decided 'to issue dinner tickets to two boys'.

In May 1913 the headmaster reported, for class V standard II:

> The first 10 minutes of each half hour to be spent in physical exercises or organised games. Object: relaxation of mental strain. The boys of this class have been weighed and measured and will be weighed and measured each month to ascertain physical and mental development.

A year later he again recorded that 'for five minutes previous to every lesson, other than those followed by drill or recreation, a form of physical exercises will be taken in class II . . . Weights of boys taken every month'. In November 1911 the boys are reported as playing football at Streatham, and during the summer holidays in the same year twenty-five boys went 'to the country by the aid of the Children's Country Holiday Fund'. Special services and special schools had also begun to be provided in London from the end of the nineteenth century; in 1915, for example, the boys' log book mentions: 'Special Examination (medical). A. Gorman. The boy has been recommended to attend a special school for deaf children.'

The curriculum and life of the school were also changing.

Payment by results had ended in the mid-1890s, although its narrowness in many respects lived on. Standards had, as we have seen, been high at Kennington in the late nineteenth century, especially in the boys' school, under the impress of Mr Broomfield, whose final connections with the school are worth noting. In 1904, when he was sixty-four and had been head teacher for thirty-five years, the L.C.C. Education Committee raised his salary from £250 to £280 a year.[8] Broomfield was, however, about to retire. The inspector's report on the school in 1904 refers to Broomfield's forthcoming retirement, and summarises the position in all three parts of the school:

London County Council.

EDUCATION DEPARTMENT.

Copy of Forwards Report of H.M. Inspector.

NON-PROVIDED SCHOOL.

KENNINGTON—
ST. MARK'S, KENNINGTON OVAL,
NATIONAL SCHOOL.

Year ended 31st October, 1904.

School No. 2,292.   BOARD OF EDUCATION,
                          WHITEHALL, LONDON, S.W.,
                                12th November, 1904.

School visited 25th and 26th March, and 21st and 22nd July, 1904.

BOYS'—" Mr. Broomfield has conducted this school for many years, and up to the present with high ability and great conscientiousness; he has largely influenced for good a long succession of scholars. His leaving his charge at Christmas must therefore be deeply felt by the Managers and assistant teachers, as well as by his boys and their parents. But it is to be hoped that the excellent tradition he has established will be maintained by his successor.

GIRLS'—" Excellent discipline and general training continue. The instruction is being given with good method and most creditable success. No pains are spared to render the teaching both useful and educational."

INFANTS'—" The school continues to be efficiently conducted."

In December 1905 the committee decided to appoint Broomfield as one of the managers, and he attended regularly until he resigned in 1910. The L.C.C. Education Committee minutes in January 1905 give details of Broomfield's successor, Mr H. Sprigge. He had been trained for two years at Cheltenham Training College, passing in the second division in the first and second year papers. He had received his 'parchment certificate' in 1889. He had certificates for 'light and shade', 'free-arm' and 'colour work', four advanced and three elementary certificates. He had been an assistant teacher for seven years. The recommended salary was £175.[9]

Mr Sprigge was to have a revealing altercation with the vicar in 1912, one which indicates the view of church–school relations still held by the vicar, and the change from the automatic deference shown by the nineteenth-century schoolmaster. The head writes:

> Vicar called: discussed service for Ascension Day. Instructed the headmaster to inform staff that a special communion service for teachers would be held after the children's service. He stated that the staff were expected to attend. Headmaster replied: that he could exercise no power over the staff in this respect. The vicar said: 'Do not argue, you must remember you are here to obey me'.

The headmaster made no further allusion to the incident, and if the vicar raised it at the committee of managers, the matter was discreetly omitted from the minutes. In 1918, against the protest of the headmistress, Mr Sprigge became Correspondent (as secretaries of management committees were designated) to the managers, a position he occupied for nearly two years. The headmaster was also a member of a number of committees in the district, including in 1912 an advisory committee of the recently created local Labour Exchange.

The points at which other teachers come to the centre of the stage in this period are mainly in relation to punishment, and two teachers in particular reveal the attitude to punishment taken by the headmaster and the L.C.C. The personality of one of them, Mr Simpson first becomes evident in October 1909, when Mr Sprigge makes a long entry in the log book:

> Message from Mr. Simpson at 2.45. Would Mr. Clayfield please come and take the class? Message sent to Mr. Simpson by me. Would Mr. Simpson please instruct the boys until Mr. Clayfield had finished the work he was doing. [The work was in connection with the prize distribution of the school.] Message from Mr. Simpson at 3.5. Would Mr. Clayfield come and take the class? The boy was asked who sent him. He replied: 'Mr. Simpson'. The boy was told to go back to his class. In a very short time Mr. Simpson came into the private room and in irate and authoritative tones asked the question 'Is Mr. Clayfield coming to take the class?' My reply was in the negative whereupon Mr. Simpson stated that he did not intend taking other master's classes and expressed the thought that he had better send the boys to play. I told Mr. Simpson that there was no need to discuss the matter and the boys were not to be sent to play. Mr. Simpson said that there was great need to discuss the matter and wished to do so. Mr. Simpson stated that the messenger had not given my message. I asked Mr. Simpson to please send the messenger to me. Mr. Simpson returned to his room and in a short time the boy came. The message should have been quite comprehensible to Mr. Simpson. The boy was sent to his class room. I was surprised to find that Mr. Simpson on returning to his room had sent the boys to play.

The precise outcome of this wrangle and Mr Simpson's challenge to the headmaster is not indicated, but there is evidence, in connection with punishment, of Mr Simpson's continued 'authoritative' manner. In November 1914, for instance, the headmaster has another log book entry:

> At 11.15 a.m. Mr. Simpson sent for the cane and book, which were sent to him. A few moments later the same boy was sent back for the larger cane. I visited Mr. Simpson's room and informed him that the small cane should be used

for young boys. Mr. Simpson said that the boy deserved
punishment but he would not punish him with the small
cane. The small cane and book were returned to the private
room. A short time had elapsed when Mr. Simpson came to
my room and asked me why I had opposed him. The
Council's regulations were referred to. Mr. Simpson asked
me to show him the regulation. The regulation was read to
Mr. Simpson. Mr. Simpson then said that he had been
degraded in the school, and that I was acting behind his
back.

In 1916 Mr Simpson was interviewed by the managers over a
complaint from a father about excessive punishment of his boy,
but the managers decided that the punishment had been in
order. In March 1917 Mr Simpson again appeared before the
managers to answer to 'a case of irregular punishment' of a
boy whom he had struck in the face, making his nose bleed.
Mr Simpson expressed his regret, 'and acknowledged the breach
of the regulations as to corporal punishment', and was warned
by the managers that 'a repetition of the breach would be of
serious consequence to him and would have to be referred to the
Council for consideration'. The headmaster again recorded in
January 1918 that 'Mr. Simpson punched a boy in the back
– reported to the L.C.C.'. At a managers' meeting in February
this

> charge of irregular punishment . . . by Mr. Simpson was
> considered, the Council Inspector being present. The boys
> mother was interviewed by the managers and she described
> the punishment as severe, stating that the boy had four
> knuckle bruises on the small of the back. Mr. Simpson was
> interviewed and he agreed that he called the boy out from
> the class and punched him twice as an example, on the
> shoulder. After consideration it was decided that as this
> was the 2nd. case within a year, that Mr. Simpson be
> censured.

Relations between the irascible Mr Simpson and the headmaster
were obviously strained. In 1915, when the latter examined Mr
Simpson's class in the analysis of simple sentences such as
'down came the boy from the top of the hill', the head recorded
that 'Mr. Simpson does not consider these to be simple sentences'.

In 1919 Mr Simpson refused to accept an instruction from the headmaster not to take singing when other classes were taking the subject.

It is interesting that Mr Simpson continued in the school with apparently nothing more than a caution and a censure, presumably because he was an efficient teacher in other respects. The position was different with Mr Clayfield, who featured in one of the incidents with Mr Simpson. The first inkling of the situation from the headmaster appears in September 1910, when he writes that 'Mr. Clayfield today struck the boy Harwood upon the head. Instruction given to Mr. Clayfield. "Under no circumstances must a boy's head be struck". A copy of this entry has been forwarded this day to the Education office.' Mr Clayfield had already, however, shown himself to be unsatisfactory in one way or another, and the previous month the managers had decided 'that Mr. Clayfield be requested to seek a post elsewhere'. This case of punishment was therefore discussed by the managers in November in a serious mood. They decided 'to terminate Mr. Clayfield's engagement at the school', giving as reasons 'unsatisfactory reports from the inspectors' and 'irregular punishment'. Even while under notice of dismissal Mr Clayfield had to be reported to the managers for another case of irregular punishment, but in the circumstances it was decided not to proceed further in the matter.

In a less sombre light appears Mr Wilson, who was engaged in 1913 as an uncertificated teacher. The managers proposed retaining him because of 'the length of service and practical skill shown by Mr. Wilson in dealing with young boys'. The L.C.C. agreed to his retention 'on the condition that he undertakes to attend a course of the Council's lectures for teachers on two evenings a week'.

In 1909 Mr Sprigge made an unexplained entry in his log book which provides a useful framework within which to see the working of the school in this period. It reads:

School Bells

9.0	Registers	Morning session
9.40	Secular work	
9.55	Registers closed	
10.40	Recreation	
11.25	Change lessons	

11.55	Lessons cease	
12.0	Dismissal	
2.0	Registers	Afternoon session
2.5	Registers closed	
2.45	Change lessons	
3.15	Recreation	
3.55	Change lessons	
4.25	Lessons cease.	Assembly for Prayers.

Other glimpses of the life of the school are possible. In 1906 the managers were asking the L.C.C. to replace '14 damaged desks in the boys' dept. by dual desks', and later in the year asked the Council 'for dual desks for the upper standards in the girls' dept.'. The headmaster in 1910 asked the managers for a 'telephone communicating from the headmaster's room to the different classrooms', but this was deferred for lack of funds. In 1912 'Mrs. Cleobury, 63 Harleyford Rd. had an interview with the managers and complained of hard balls being continually hit over into her garden, to the danger and annoyance of the residents'. It was decided 'that in future no hard balls should be used in the playground'. In 1911 the headmaster mentions that 'gasmen attended to the globes, mantles, etc.', and in the following year the managers began to be concerned about minor road accidents occurring when the children left school – and they asked the Council 'whether steps could not be taken to notify motorists of the fact of a school being situated at the corner of Harleyford Rd.'.

Although changes in the teaching and curriculum took place in this period, there is not the same preoccupation with teaching methods in the records that we shall see in the period between the wars. A hint of the direction in which the teachers were being drawn comes in 1910, when an H.M.I. visited the school and 'suggested an alteration in the method of teaching "Poetry". There should be no simultaneous work. Boys in Class I should be allowed to select their own poetry.' The boys' department was reorganised in 1911 into five classes, and greater specialisation was introduced:

Singing:	Mr Maynard	Classes	I. II. III.
Algebra:	Mr Simpson	,,	I. II.
History:	Mr Steele	,,	I. II. III.

A modern language, presumably French, was being taught in the school in 1907 (though there is no mention of it in the school's own records). The L.C.C. Education Committee received a report in that year from a sub-committee, recommending that this foreign language at St Mark's be discontinued at the end of the year, and the time allotted to 'English and other kindred educational subjects'.[10] 'Handwork' was introduced in 1914. Football, as we have seen, was being played by the boys in 1911, and Saturday cricket was being played in 1915. Swimming was a regular activity in the school, and in 1914 there is mention in the girls' log book of tennis: 'girls began to play tennis at Vauxhall Park'.

The following report for 1912 by an L.C.C. inspector gives a detailed picture of the school at work. It contains comments on science, and it is interesting that in the same year there is the first reference in the headmaster's log book to the receipt of 'science stock'. Apart from Mr Simpson's new responsibilities for algebra, and the occasional presence of arithmetic in a list of one sort or another, mathematics goes undiscussed in this period.

BOYS.—(1) The school is organised in five classes.

(2) The schemes of work are well drawn up, are suitable and effectively taught.

(3) Since the last inspection (1911) considerable progress has been made and the work as a whole now reaches a very good level.

(4) Mr. Chesterton reports 'Physical Exercises in three classes as very good and satisfactory in the classes taught by Mr. Wilson and Mr. Steele.' He points out 'that these two teachers are unqualified.'

(5) Mr. Todd reports on the Science: 'The boys answer very well and the instruction is made thoroughly practical. The syllabus needs some revision and simplification.'

(6) Mr. Clarke reports on the Drawing: 'Much of the work is now very good, especially in classes 1, 2 and 5. In class 3 the subjects set are often too ambitious. In class 4 more attention must be given to observation.'

(7) The suggestions made in the Handicraft report will receive attention.

COMBINED GIRLS AND INFANTS.—(1) This school consists

of two departments, Girls' and Infants', under one head mistress.

(2) The infants are taught in two rooms, there being two classes with two teachers in one room, and one class in the other.

The Girls' department is taught in three rooms and each mistress has two standards to teach. The work is thus carried on under difficult conditions.

(3) Of the three divisions of the school, only one may be characterised as good—viz.: standards IV and V.

(4) The first division taught by Miss Apted may as a whole be called fairly good, but many of the girls in the oral subjects are very dull and inert. Miss Apted works well herself, prepares her lessons well, but the results of her work are not commensurate with her efforts. She must try to infuse a spirit of work in the girls in her class.

(5) The lower division, taught by Miss Obee, is only very fair. She herself works well, but the work would be more effective if her discipline were stronger.

(6) Mr. Todd reporting on the Science teaching, says: 'Instruction is given in general Hygiene and Nature Study, but there is a lack of that definiteness and thoroughness which is essential to make it of real use to the girls. The syllabus should be revised and built up on broader and more experimental lines.'

(7) Miss Jones reporting on the Needlework, says: 'The Needlework scheme has been carefully planned and the instruction given is very thorough.' She suggests (a) the supply of a sewing machine: (b) that cutting-out on material should be done in classes below standard IV; (c) that the making of garments should be started earlier in the year.

(8) Mr. Clarke reports on the Drawing as follows: 'Improvement continues. The renderings with the brush are, as a rule, satisfactory. The Crayon drawings are less crude than formerly.'

(9) The Infants' section of the school is bright and well taught.

In 1911 a prize scheme is outlined by the headmaster (prize distributions were regular annual events), including prizes for boys who excelled in arithmetic, reading, writing, spelling, recitation, drawing, history, geography and science. There was a prize for the boy who made the greatest progress, and one for the top boy in each class.

Between 1906 and 1918 fifteen boys won scholarships for secondary schools, four for Borough Polytechnic and one for Battersea Polytechnic, two to Mercers' School, one to Alleyn's, one to Westminster City and one to the 'School of Engineering'. Five boys also won junior county scholarships – an outcome of the new scholarship 'ladder' to secondary education which had come into existence. Even in the last decades of the nineteenth century a small number of such scholarships were available in some areas for able elementary school children to go to grammar schools. Under the 'free place' regulations of 1907 local authority secondary schools were required to make 25 per cent of their intake free-place pupils, under a scholarship system for which elementary school pupils could compete. London's county scholarship system had been inaugurated in 1893, when up to 600 scholarships a year (with free tuition for two years and maintenance grants) were made available. This had increased to over 2,000 by 1905 (with free education up to 14-plus, renewable for a further two years, and improved maintenance grants). By 1910, partly as a result of the 1907 regulations, London had 7,880 scholarship holders.[11] In these changing circumstances the scholarship record at Kennington does not suggest that in this respect at least Mr Broomfield's 'excellent tradition' was, as the inspector had hoped, maintained by his successor. Between 1913 and 1918 the girls had half or whole day holidays for Empire Day and Ascension Day, the Shakespeare tercentenary, military successes by old boys, and the armistice; they had three half-days when boys won 'athletic distinctions', but only twice do they appear to have celebrated the boys' scholarship successes.

The First World War made surprisingly little impression on the school, if the log books and managers' minutes are anything to judge by. The first reference in the minutes is in June 1915, when Mr Wilson wrote to the managers to say that he had been called up for service with the National Reserve (another teacher enlisted the following year). The headmaster's first, and indirect, reference is also in 1915, when a rifle club was formed: 'The range is in the crypt of St. Mark's Church. The boys are taught firing during the intervals of school sessions.' At the same time, presumably at least in part because of the war, the garden adjoining the girls' school was 'divided into plots by the first class boys. Each plot has been sown with vegetable seeds. Instruction is given in Nature Study.' The outcome of these latter two ventures is not described, but the crypt of St Mark's Church was to appear again in the minutes of the managers in November 1917:

> A letter was read from the Council on air raid precautions and after careful discussion and consideration it was decided that the children should be mustered and immediately marched under the teacher's escort to the crypt of the Church when a warning of an impending raid was received.

The vicar and his wife 'very kindly agreed to being responsible for the opening of the church gates and helping to receive the children'. Apart from the occasional half holidays when former pupils won military distinctions the only other reference of substance to the war occurs in the confrontation Mr Simpson had with the managers in 1916. He had been accused by a parent, in fact, not only of excessively punishing his son, but also of 'lack of patriotism'. The managers decided that 'there was no lack of patriotism in Mr. Simpson's remarks', but suggested that these had been 'perhaps a little indiscreet to one who had recently lost a son in the war'. On 11 November 1918, the headmaster wrote simply that the inspector had sent a message to close the school for the afternoon on account of the armistice.

1918–39

The two principal areas of interest in the life of Kennington School between the wars relate to new teaching methods and the beginnings of a reorganisation in the educational system.

The 'new' or 'progressive' educational ideas of the late nineteenth and early twentieth centuries had already had some influence on the school: as we have seen, handwork had been introduced, experiments with regular physical activity throughout the school day had been conducted, with the object of 'relaxation of mental strain', and the H.M.I. had 'suggested' the dropping of 'simultaneous' work in poetry. The early 1920s, however, show a brisk increase in the pressures towards new ideas in elementary school teaching, and at Kennington this is reflected notably in the girls' school. In September 1921 there was a conference of senior staff, following one of head-teachers: 'subject, individual and sectional teaching'. In March 1923 the infant mistresses visited Stockwell College infants' school 'to see individual work and vertical classification', and the following month spent an afternoon at a 'sample room . . . to see individual apparatus'. The infant teachers, it is clear, were anxious to keep abreast of new ideas about grouping and individual work, and in 1930, for example, were visiting Telferscot Road Infants School in Balham, 'to observe the sentence method of teaching reading'. In November and December 1932 an infant teacher went for eight sessions to a college of physical education on an infant physical training course.

It was not only the infant teachers, however, who were involved in moves towards more indivualised teaching, and in June 1923 all the staff of the girls' department 'from 4.20 p.m. visited the rooms of the National Society and heard a lecture on "Individual Work in the Schools" '. The head and her staff were also investigating other ideas. In May 1923, for instance, a conference was held in the headteacher's room from 2–3 p.m. on geography teaching: 'the staff of the girls' school was present, and Miss Welford, Geog. Lecturer, Stockwell Training College spoke of new methods in geography'. Six months later the head attended a headteachers' conference at Brixton Central School, on 'the teaching and testing of reading in senior schools'. Early the following year she went to a conference on 'choice of books' and 'the circulating reading scheme'.

New aspects of teaching can be seen in other developments. A feature of the Empire Day celebrations in 1923, for example, was 'the introduction of the gramophone to convey a message to the children from the King and Queen. The record was subscribed for by the girls and infants by means of a farthing collection. The cost – 5s/6d would eventually become a donation to children's hospitals through the gramophone company.' The school did not at this stage possess its own gramophone, but in 1929 the headmistress reports: 'a gramophone and records came into use in the school. These were purchased through the L.C.C. by money raised at the jumble sale and other voluntary subscriptions.' In 1923 the school held its first open day, when

L

parents were invited in the afternoon to see a display of children's work (this was just before the Christmas holidays, and was described as 'an unqualified success'). In 1925 the first party of girls went on a school journey, to Broadstairs (and others followed regularly, to the Isle of Wight, Hastings and elsewhere). The interest in new ideas in the girls' school continued. In February 1937, for example, the headmistress and one of the staff went to the Victoria cinema to see a film on physical education. In December of the same year the headmistress went twice in one week to see a preview of educational films, and a party of forty girls made three visits to see educational films.

An interesting side-light on the school's relationship to the nation-wide movement of educational ideas in the 1920s is the coincidence that one of the outstanding figures in this new movement, T. Percy Nunn, had contact with the school in 1920, the year in which he published his famous *Education: its data and first principles*, which summarised the 'play way', individualised methods in education. The headmaster reported in November of that year that 'Dr. T. Percy Nunn, V. Principal of the London Day Training College, visited the school with a view to making arrangements for students of the College to attend this school for teaching practice . . . whilst the Kennington Rd. School was closed'. A month later he again visited the school to ask 'if it would be possible to continue the attendance of students of the London Day Training College'. The visits of Nunn, and the presence of his students, as well as the other developments we have seen are no more than hints of the climate of opinion surrounding elementary schools; this was the first time in the history of the school that there had been serious and sustained pressures on the staff not just to apply efficiently but also to examine and change their curriculum and teaching methods. Perhaps one of the most symbolic entries in the girls' log book in this respect was the first mention, in June 1924, of a staff meeting: 'A staff meeting was held in the Hd Thr's room from 3.45 p.m. to discuss outstanding school matters, the summer programme of activities and educational items connected with the work.'

From the L.C.C. report of 1927 it may be deduced that the boys' school was more traditional in its work (there were no school journeys or visits, arithmetic included too few problems, and in science there was too little first-hand observation). The report (by three of the Council's district inspectors and the physical education organiser) comments about the school in general:

> Kennington Oval school is agreeably situated and draws upon a fairly good population. Its internal arrangements are convenient, and it has an excellent playground. There are four classes, the first of which is taught by the head master.
>
> The school has a distinct character of its own, and the general tone and feeling among the boys is thoroughly good. The work is vigorous and lively; but, owing to staff limitations, there are no outside activities, such as school journeys or educational visits. The school, however, does very well in Sports and Swimming.
>
> Clear and sensible syllabuses have been drawn up by the head master, very commendable attention being paid to the needs of the older and brighter boys in the top class.

The more detailed comments are worth reproducing in full as an interesting commentary on the state of the school, and as an indication of the elementary school curriculum and aspects of the teaching of different subjects of this period:

> *English.*—The English is, in general, quite good. The books containing written work showed intelligent choice of matter and careful revision, and tests set at the time of inspection were creditably done. In oral work the boys were intelligent and responsive, those in the top class being specially agreeable. Something of their general intelligence and ease of manner could profitably be caught by the rather less flexible class below them. The third class (Standards III. and IV.) is very well taught. Class 4, the lowest, under the care of an efficient, serious and hard-working mistress, suffers a little from its constitution. Girls corresponding in age to most of the boys here are in an Infants' class doing Infant school work, and going home at 4 o'clock. The boys are in a boys' school, and senior school work is expected from them.
>
> *Arithmetic.*—The syllabus defines separate courses of work for the upper and lower divisions in each class, but the working of the scheme in the second class is at present

interfered with by the absence of the master during two lessons in the week on other duties (Swimming and Games); hence a good deal of the work so far has been taken with the class as a whole.

The teaching is effective, and the results, as revealed by oral and written tests, are in general satisfactory. The teachers of the lowest two classes are very thorough, both in their methods and in their efforts to raise the standard of accuracy. In the second class the written work includes too few problems; in the first, the claims of care in presentation have been sacrificed, to some extent, to those of speed. The boys in this class showed to better advantage in oral answering than in written work.

At present the lowest class is without text-books, and many copies of those in use in other classes are badly worn. The school contemplates an early change in the text-books used. When new books have been supplied, their consistent use throughout the school should prove of definite advantage.

Science and Nature Study.—The scheme of work for the lowest class is based on a book which in itself is quite suitable for general reading, and the material is supplemented in the oral lessons. It would be better, however, to adopt a scheme which gave the boys greater opportunities for first-hand observation in the open spaces near the school. The scheme of work for the next two classes is a course of general elementary Science. The school possesses a small quantity of apparatus, and the teacher of the third class makes full use of this in carrying out interesting and illuminating demonstrations. The lack of demonstration in Class 2 tends to deprive the work of value and interest. Science is, unfortunately, omitted from the curriculum of class 1, and its reintroduction is desirable.

As one classroom is empty, it is possible that arrangements might be made for some kind of practical work for the older boys. For this, additional apparatus would be required.

Geography.—Fairly good geographical knowledge was shown by the boys of the first class. The teaching is regional, and, as much time is devoted to such matters as rainbelts, etc., the boys were tested, as an experiment, on topography.

They did quite well, and filled in a blank map without gross errors. In the second class the work showed less conviction on the part of the teacher and less acquirements on the part of the boys. In the third class, the teacher gave a good lesson on map-reading, and here a very pleasing feature was the clear and precise (if rather memorised) answers of the boys. Where regional geography prevails, care should be taken to see that the word "region" is neither uttered nor written as "regent." In the fourth class there were definite indications of intelligent work, much illustrative matter having been collected.

History.—This subject is less well done than the Geography. The work does not rise above ordinary routine lessons, and there seems to be little in the way of wall-charts or other illustrative material. The first class showed some knowledge of the Hanoverian period, but there was a tendency to confuse the '15 and the '45 rebellions, and the Young Pretender was thought to be the son of Charles II. Charles I. was alleged to be a Roman Catholic by twelve boys, a Presbyterian by six, a Protestant (or Puritan) by five, and a member of the Church of England by three. It is difficult to see how any real understanding of the seventeenth century can be derived from such a state of confusion. The boys of the second class, tested orally, answered well: but there was no connection between the History Reader and the scheme followed, and no evidence of any illustrative material having been used. The work in the two lower classes calls for no special remarks.

It should be said generally that, where written tests were set, there was a low standard of composition and spelling. Practice in the proper setting down of answers to questions should be regularly given.

Music.—The Singing is vigorous, but a little too violent to be pleasing. Sight-reading should be practised and the elements of the staff-notation should be taught.

Drawing.—The drawing of the school is, on the whole, satisfactory, the best work being that done with the youngest children, where there is more feeling and a little less mechanism than in some other classes.

Physical Education.—The results in Classes 1, 3, and 4 are good. In Class 2, an earnest effort has been made, but the

instruction is not altogether in accord with modern requirements. Throughout the school the boys work keenly and
show a spirit of response. In addition, each class has a period
for organised games, and the three top groups take
Swimming.

In out-of-school activities Cricket is taken up very
successfully, the school for many years occupying a
prominent position in local competitions.

The report concluded that the school had 'many praiseworthy
features', including its 'remarkable record of successes in games
and competitive sports'. It praised the careful recording of the
'peculiarities, circumstances and achievements' of the boys,
past and present, and the interest taken in their careers after
leaving school. The inspectors thought that 'the school is lacking
perhaps in repose and refinement; but it clearly makes definite
efforts for the personal good of its charges, and, in spite of
difficulties caused by its organisation, it does efficient and
creditable work'. At their next meeting the managers expressed
their regret that the inspectors thought the school 'lacking
perhaps in repose and refinement'; the managers were not of
that opinion, and applauded the efforts of the head and the
staff in 'the difficult conditions under which the school work
is carried on'. By 1938, it may be noted, at least the matter of
visits had been put right. The following took place, for example,
during the autumn term of that year:

40 boys to the Royal Academy of Dramatic Art, Gower St,
   to see 'The Merchant of Venice'.
14 boys taken to the Albert Hall to a final rehearsal of Sir
   Henry Wood's jubilee performance.
33 boys to a demonstration by London Fire Brigade.
Class 3 – a lantern lecture.
Class 1 – taken to 'educational films'.
Class 1 B – taken to Horniman's Museum.
Class 1 A – taken to Horniman's Museum for a lecture on
   transport.
On December 22nd the boys were given bags of sweets, a
   toffee apple and an orange, and were entertained with
   conjuring tricks.

The number of teachers in the school fluctuated, with the

L.C.C. adjusting the number of assistant masters or mistresses to the number of children on roll. The number of boys in the school declined in the early 1930s, and the Council responded accordingly by cutting the staff to the headteacher plus two assistants. A letter to the chairman of the managers in April 1935 justifying the reduction comments:

that the present actual roll is just over 100 and there is no reason to assume that this roll will be greatly exceeded after Easter. In these circumstances a four class organisation could not be justified and it was necessary under the Council's rules to make a reduction. If, however, the actual roll after Easter, 1935, exceeds 132, the head master may make application for a floating staff teacher.

The log book for the period 1936–8 shows that the boys' school had, in fact, a 'head teacher in charge of a class', two permanent assistants and one 'floating staff teacher'. In the girls' school in January 1937, on the other hand, there were five permanent assistant mistresses and the headmistress. Three months later, the latter writes: 'School reopened after the Easter holidays with a total roll of 283. An extra class of girls was formed and added accommodation – a room in the boys' dept. is in use. Staff – 1 head – 5 permanent mistresses and 1 floating teacher.' The L.C.C., taking advantage of the declining population of inner London areas (including Lambeth), was at this point engaged in efforts to reduce class sizes. It pointed out to the Kennington managers that its aim was a maximum of 48 children in infant classes and 40 in others, and that it had succeeded in bringing 95 per cent of its schools within this framework. 'Having regard to the fall in the roll of the boys' department,' it suggested, 'it may now be practicable to allocate one of the rooms in this department for the use of the girls' section. This would enable the accommodation of the larger class rooms in this section to be reduced to 40 each.' In 1933 the two infant classrooms at Kennington had had 48 places each, and the three girls' classrooms 42, 48 and 54 places.

About the teachers themselves during this period a little information can be gleaned from the managers' minutes. In May 1919 the managers were still asking the L.C.C. 'whether steps had been taken to release Mr. Maynard from the Army in order to secure his services for the school'. In the same year

Mrs Florence Pratt was appointed as an assistant mistress in the girls' department, and the minutes provide a cameo description of her:

> The following particulars were ascertained: –
> Husband: at Ministry of Munitions formerly 'clerk'.
> Home at Lowestoft. Health good.
> Taught shorthand at a boarding school.
> Fond of studying for studying's sake.
> The headmistress recommended appointment. She said 'Mrs. Pratt appeared to be fond of work for the work's sake. Teachers must study in these days'. The manner, attitude and intonation of Mrs. Pratt had impressed the head mistress.

Mrs Pratt's interview and appointment reveal as much about the views of the headmistress and the committee as about those of Mrs Pratt herself. When the head resigned in 1922 the committee interviewed eleven candidates, including Mrs Pratt – who was highly recommended by the head. The committee selected Mrs Pratt as 'the most suitable candidate for the position notwithstanding the fact that Mrs. Pratt has had no college training'. They believed her to be a 'well educated woman', and – again indicating the prevailing educational atmosphere – recorded that 'her personal charm, her refined attitude, her up-to-date and progressive methods and her kind and inspiring manner commended themselves most highly to the managers and warranted her appointment'. The L.C.C., however, were not impressed by Mrs Pratt's qualifications – or lack of them – for the post, and its Teaching Staff Sub-Committee recommended 'that on educational grounds consent should not be given'. Since all appointments had to be endorsed by the L.C.C. the school re-interviewed, and appointed a candidate from the Stockwell Practising School, one who had not been previously interviewed.

As much interest centres in this period on the caretaker as on the teaching staff. Nine candidates for the vacant post of caretaker were considered in 1924. The present occupation of one of the candidates was given as caretaker, one as assistant caretaker; the occupation of one was 'casual', one was temporary clerk with the L.C.C., one was in post office work, one worked for the gas company, two were unemployed, and the occupation of one is not shown. The successful candidate was one of the youngest (occupation 'casual'), was ex-navy, his father had been a schoolkeeper, and was a gas engineer. By this time the caretaker was occupying the major part of what had been the headmaster's house (part being used for school purposes; the other house, less one room used by the headmistress, was rented out). In 1932 a subsequent caretaker was sacked for inefficiency, and he was formally instructed to vacate the premises on December 16. The post was advertised and 300 applications were received (no doubt a reflection of the level of unemployment at this period); ten applicants were interviewed. Trouble with regaining possession of the house was obviously anticipated, and a solicitor was retained in the event of having to go to court. This did in fact prove necessary, and at Lambeth Police Court on 21 January the outgoing caretaker was given twenty-one days in which to leave the premises.

The health of the children continued to be of major importance. When the school dentist visited Kennington in December 1935 he inspected eighty boys, and twenty-three were declared 'clean'; thirty, the head comments, would be a good fraction. This was a period of intensive national efforts to improve children's teeth, and Kennington reflected the national concern. The school Care Committee continued to play a prominent part in the life of the school. A letter from the L.C.C. appointing a new member of the Kennington Care Committee in 1937 explained: 'you probably already know the work that the Care Committee do in connection with the feeding of necessitous children, the following up of medical work and the advice given to children when they leave school ... '. The last phrase indicates a function of the Care Committee which was not to be taken over by a Youth Employment Service until after the Second World War.

An important fact in the discussion of the school in this period is the significant social change that had taken place in the surrounding district since the late nineteenth century. Throughout the nineteenth century, it has been said, 'North Lambeth became slummier and slummier.'[12] This is certainly true of Kennington at the end of the century and the early decades of the twentieth. In the early 1930s the L.C.C. decided on a housing scheme for the area. The managers were told that this was imminent at their meeting in December 1933, and by the following June it was reported that 'houses in Kennington Oval and Clayton St. [a street off the Oval] had been pulled down, and two blocks of flats were being built, one immediately outside the school ... which will house many families from a slum clearance scheme when completed'. By 1938 it was reported that 'work of the Care Committee Secretary was increasing owing to the poorer type of child who now attended the schools, coming from the L.C.C. flats'. This was an extremely concentrated and substantial housing development, and it is likely that the problem was not so much the 'poorer type of child' as the increased number of such children, and the continued outward migration of lower-middle-class families. The only guide to the influence of these changes on the social composition of the school are the records of the occupations of the children's parents (and these records exist for only very limited periods). In the eighteen months from June 1925 to the end of 1926 the girls' school admitted children whose parent or guardian gave the following occupations: retailer (6), business man, clerk, bus conductor, wine merchant, manager Surrey Tavern, silverer, disabled soldier, horse keeper, retired publican (now sweet shop owner), coffee stall worker, actor, pensioner (2), salesman – market, repairing motors, milkman, sells flowers, draughtsman, electrician, repairer of watches, stonemason, engine driver, chauffeur, compositor, engineer, boot trade, meat cold store keeper, Covent Garden – fruit and vegetable. From the beginning of 1927 and for the rest of the 1930s the girls' admission registers only rarely record the parent's occupation (the handful of cases include factory hand, Lieutenant killed in war, labourer, housewife (3), Watney's brewery ...).

As for the earlier period there is difficulty in interpreting some of these descriptions, but the majority fall into lower middle class, skilled or semi-skilled worker categories. In 1936 and 1937, after the slum clearance development, admissions to the boys' school showed the following parental occupations: window cleaner (2), messenger (2), labourer (14), timber, electrician (2), docker, painter, motoring – transport, wig decker, brewery porter, Covent Garden, cook – Cafe Royal Regent St, unemployed (2), carpenter (2), publican, roadsman, wrestler, painter and paperhanger, printer, newsagent's assistant, grain thrower, tailor, manager SR Restaurant Victoria, railway LMS, liftman, potter, builder's man, postman, LPTB.

This list suggests, though there are difficulties in establishing comparisons, that there had been an increase in the number of children from unskilled working-class families; the number of children from shopkeeping and similar families had declined, and it is probable that the redevelopment of the area had produced a greater social homogeneity, with lower-middle-class families moving further south in Lambeth, or to outer suburbs.

The Kennington Oval rehousing scheme involved 1,264 'tenement and block dwellings', and the L.C.C. estimated that 1,500 new school places would be required. The Council announced its intention to provide a new public elementary school for about 900 children in Bowling Green Street (not far from St Mark's School). At a meeting in September 1934 the managers expressed their agitation, drafted a protest, and appealed to other voluntary schools in the area, and to the Diocesan Director of Religious Education, for support. The other schools and the diocese declined to back the protest, and the St Mark's managers did not send it. The L.C.C. explained in reply to an enquiry what the number of children coming into the area was likely to be, and it was realised that 'the new school could not be built for two or three years, and meanwhile people would be coming into the area, and our school might reasonably expect to fill up and become established'. In March 1936 the headmaster proposed and the managers agreed that they 'should send a circular letter to the occupants of the new flats drawing attention to the Oval Schools'.

The difficulties, particularly in the boys' school, were great, not only because of low numbers. Mr Sprigge had retired in 1935, after thirty years at the school, and his successor stayed only two years (being given immediate release when he requested it, to take up an appointment in the Musical Instrument and Radio Technology Department of the Northern Polytechnic). Population turnover had made a profound impact on the life of the school. The diocesan inspector summed up the situation in April 1937 when he described the boys' school as going through a difficult period, partly because of the head's departure and partly because 'new entrants of various types and attainments have been coming in, and there has not yet been time to assimilate and train them in the school's traditions'. The local population and the school had, it would seem, both become less 'various'.

Boys from the school did, nevertheless, occasionally win scholarships, though at a declining rate. Fifteen had been won in the period 1906–18; thirteen were won in the period 1919–35 (and in addition two former pupils were reported in 1926 as having gone to Oxford and Cambridge). There are also from the 1920s occasional references to girls winning county scholarships, the first mentioned being in 1920. In 1938, for example, two awards were announced for girls at the school; the parents of one 'withdrew her from the scholarship award' and the other one was taken up at Mary Datchelor School, Camberwell.

The prize scheme previously mentioned was codified for the boys' school by Mr Sprigge, probably between 1920 and 1922. The details are of interest, in their expression of the interpretation of schooling for social ends – as explicit in its way as the nineteenth-century statements about the purpose of elementary education:

PRIZE SCHEME.

There are five classes in this school with two sections to each class. There are two terms during the year, and promotions are made from grade to grade each term.

1. Progress and Industry are the chief considerations in the selection of prize winners.
2. Regular and punctual attendance have an influence on the selection of prize winners.
3. Prize winners should be boys who are capable of setting a good example to others.
4. A certain standard must be reached in order to gain a prize.
5. Consideration will be given to boys who show special aptitude in any particular subject of the curriculum.
6. The top boy of each class, subject to clause 11, will be awarded a prize.
7. A prize will be given, subject to clause 11, to the boy who gains the greatest number of rings in each class during the year.
8. The most popular boy in the school may be awarded a prize.
9. Headmaster's Prize—
   Awarded to the boy who shows most promise of becoming a good and worthy citizen.
   (Civis Romanus sum)

10. In cases of outstanding merit, a prize for Sports may be awarded.
11. No prize will be awarded to a boy whose conduct is unsatisfactory.

There is little reference to punishment in this period. In 1937 one of the teachers had to answer a parent's complaint about the punishment of his child for persistent late arrival – on three occasions the boy had been stopped from going to swimming, and once he had been made to stand on the form for an hour. When he broke a ruler 'by wanton carelessness' the teacher had given him a choice of being caned or 'being cut out of cricket', and he had chosen the latter – though the teacher subsequently waived the punishment. 'There is no suggestion of bitterness in the boy at all,' the teacher wrote to the Education Officer. 'He goes to Clapham on an errand, on about three afternoons each week, and shows an obvious eagerness to get his instructions early enough to enable him to travel on the railway with me.' The drama of this event is somewhat different from some of those of the previous period.

Occasionally other aspects of the school and of the outside world, trivial and serious, can be glimpsed in the records. In 1931 'a tramp was discovered in the girls lavatories – he had slept there. Police interviewed him and sent on.' In May 1926 the diocesan inspector had to come alone and inspect both departments of the school, being unable to obtain assistance because of the General Strike. A letter from the L.C.C. was also read to the managers after the strike, in which it 'thanked the teachers for duty rendered during the period of industrial disturbance' – though there is no evidence that the Kennington School had been unduly disturbed. In 1936 the boys' log book reports half- or whole-day closures for the funeral of George V, Ash Wednesday, Ascension Day, Empire Day, prize distribution, the Lord Mayor's procession, and Christmas shopping. On 8 May a decision was taken to cancel the Commonwealth Day ceremony the following day 'in view of international situation', and it was decided instead that the headmaster would give 'a suitable short talk on the *realities* of the position today' to the assembled school. In the same year realities nearer at hand can be glimpsed when, on 21 December, '20 boys – whose fathers were out-of-work were taken by headmaster to Olympia Circus to see full-dress rehearsal. By invitation of Bertram Mills and

Mayor of Lambeth and permission of L.C.C. Left school at 3.30 . . .' for Olympia, where they were also given tea.

Other memorable events in the life of the school included a severe winter in 1928–9 (when, in February, the children 'huddled together in one corner of each room – warmed in relays', and the headmistress described Europe as being 'in the throes of Arctic weather unknown for 200 years'); the introduction of a school cap for the boys in November 1937 (54 were sold in two months, and 50 more were ordered in September 1938); and the occasion in June 1933 when a tramcar overturned and knocked down the railings in front of the girls' school (the next reported incident of this kind was to be in 1949, when the culprit was a Watney's Brewery lorry, which knocked down the fence and a tree).

A minute of the managers in 1920 points towards the main dilemma that was to face the school in the 1920s and 1930s – the implications of plans to reorganise the whole education system. It was decided in 1920 to recommend suitable pupils 'to attend the Archbishop Temple's School Lambeth Rd. when it becomes a C. of E. Central School'. In the late nineteenth century there had been pressures for what came to be known as 'post-primary'[13] (various kinds of senior, central or higher-grade) education within the elementary system, offering in one form or another 'higher' or 'further' education for children unable to transfer to secondary schools. By the 1920s local authorities had experimented with a variety of such schools, including Central Schools in London from the beginning of the 1910s, designed to provide a higher education for able, senior pupils from elementary schools. The problem for the voluntary authorities was going to be – would they be able to compete in the provision of such education?

In 1925 and 1926 the managers and the L.C.C. inspectors were trying to devise a scheme for improving the organisation of the Kennington School, proposing to remove boys from the infant department. Although this was agreed on more than one occasion, the matter was frequently postponed (one of the problems being that it would result in a down-grading of the girls' department). This kind of problem was overtaken by larger ones, however, after the publication in 1926 of the report of the Board of Education Consultative Committee (the Hadow Committee), *The Education of the Adolescent*. This report, reflecting growing demands for 'secondary education for all' since the end of the First World War, put forward a number of simple precepts:

> Primary education should be regarded as ending at about the age of 11+ ... All normal children should go forward to some form of post-primary education ... At the age of 11+ pupils from primary schools should normally be transferred to a different school ... It is desirable that education up to the age of 11+ should be known by the general name of Primary Education, and education after that age by the general name of Secondary Education.

Traditional 'secondary' schools should be known as Grammar Schools. Schools of the type of existing selective or non-selective central schools should be known as Modern Schools (and where these were not available and children stayed on at their primary schools, there were to be Senior Classes, or Senior Tops, as they were often called). The essential theme, that 'some form of post-primary education should be made available for all normal children between the ages of 11 and 14', implied a major reorganisation.[14] The scheme did not immediately become the subject of new legislation, but the Board of Education supported the Hadow view that 'a new stage in education should begin at about the age of 11+ and that wherever possible, children should be transferred at that age to a new school'.

The problem posed by the report, it explained, was 'that of the adaptation of the existing Elementary School system so that all the older children, not a selected few, may receive an education suited to their age and special needs'.[15]

London, like many local authorities, was anxious to try to implement such a scheme, but there were obstacles, not least of them financial. For the voluntary schools the problems were acute. In March 1927 the Kennington managers expressed support for a scheme for non-provided Central schools for girls, but there the matter rested. For the voluntary schools extensive reorganisation, involving among other things new buildings, was impracticable. No scheme of Hadow reorganisation was possible unless the voluntary bodies could build large numbers of post-primary schools, or unless they were prepared to abandon their senior pupils to a new form of local authority secondary schools – or unless a government was willing to confront the churches and end the dual system.

The way towards a solution was provided by the 1936
Education Act, which proposed to re-introduce building grants
to voluntary bodies, at the same time as raising the school
leaving age from fourteen to fifteen (though with the enormous
loophole of exemptions for 'beneficial employment'). Southwark
Diocesan Schools Association printed a summary of the act,
giving advice to managers, and headed 'Very Important'. Each
member of the Kennington managers was given a copy. Under
the act grants could be given for enlarging voluntary schools or
providing new ones, in order to make provision for senior
children. The summary made it clear that when proposals for
building schemes were submitted (during 1938, and to be
implemented by September 1940), they must:

(a) Give increased accommodation for SENIOR children,
    rendered necessary by the raising of the school age,

                            or

(b) Improve the organisation of education for SENIOR
    children in the area,

                            or

(c) Provide accommodation required for practical or
    advanced instruction for SENIOR children.

The proposed building grants to the managers for these purposes
were to be between 50 and 75 per cent. The Board of Education
issued a circular requesting authorities which had not already
done so to plan to reorganise their schools on Hadow lines.
From this point onwards the reorganisation issue was to be of
salient importance to the Kennington School. London was now
plunged into a detailed appraisal of all its schools, with a view
to implementing the Hadow principles.

The first consequence for Kennington was that when its
headmaster left in 1937 the L.C.C. refused to allow a successor
to be appointed. Until the new scheme was drawn up and
discussed with the Church authorities, the Education Officer
asked 'that the managers will postpone consideration of the
appointment of a new head teacher', and in July an assistant
master was appointed to take temporary charge of the school.
The diocesan authorities advised the managers 'to draw up a
scheme of school organisation rather than wait for the Local
Educational Council's scheme'. A long discussion took place
at the managers' meeting in June (to which the headmistress

was called in) 'on the possibilities of reorganisation of this
school. The feeling of the meeting was that a school with a
senior top should be the aim.' The situation was different when
the committee met the following month:

> A scheme was submitted by the L.C.C. embracing Vauxhall
> St Peter's, Kennington Oval St Mark's, Lambeth St
> Saviour's and St Mary the Less by which it was proposed
> that St Mark's should become a Junior Mixed School . . .
> The managers strongly disliked the idea of losing their senior
> boys and girls and it was decided that everything should be
> done to press for senior girls to remain, it being realised
> that the senior boys would have to be given up.

The meeting was told that the bishop of the diocese had convened
a meeting of Church school managers to 'consider the position
that has arisen through the L.C.C. pressing the Church to
reorganise her schools in accordance with the Hadow Report'.
Representatives of the managers attended two such meetings
in July, one for the diocese and one for the three schools proposed
to be grouped. The managers expressed various anxieties,
including the likely loss of senior children to L.C.C. schools
and the loss of infants 'brought by seniors'; local parental
preference for the Oval School and its tradition; staff problems
(were they to remain and adapt themselves to another kind of
teaching, or be summarily transferred to another school?); the
number of girls in the school was increasing; the new scheme
would leave rooms unused. At a meeting of managers of Church
of England schools in Lambeth the proposal was put forward
in discussion that the Kennington School should become
'a senior girls', junior mixed and infants' school'. The underlying theme of the meeting was that Hadow reorganisation
was now inevitable, and the meeting was told of

> the probability that in 15 or 20 years' time the non-provided
> schools although hitherto, as a result of reorganisation in
> Council schools, certain of them benefited by increased rolls,
> will have to face a gradual freezing out as senior and junior
> schools are accepted by parents as a standard form of
> education.

Decisions were taken in 1938. The managers' minutes for
October explain that 'it was surmised and had been discussed

M

by a representative committee that Salamanca Schools would be selected for the new Senior School in conjunction with Holy Trinity Lambeth SE1. The Oval Schools it was thought would become Infants and Junior Mixed.' The headmistress wrote in December that 'a decision of joint managers of Church schools was made for this group, making this Girls and Ifts dept. into Infants and Junior Mixed in the subsequent re-organisation'.

In September 1938, however, the headmistress had already recorded the impact of the growing international crisis on the school:–'War crisis. Nearly half the scholars were prepared daily for a week of evacuation. Two parents' meetings were held in the school to explain the scheme.' In the boys' school on 28 and 29 September 'the whole party was ready in school with all luggage, food, and gas masks, to proceed via Vauxhall Station immediately. On Friday the 30th, "No evacuation today" was announced, and most of the luggage was taken home.' A year later the international crisis resulted in the opening of the school during the late summer holidays for evacuation rehearsals. On 1 September the acting headmaster wrote that 'the school party [17 teachers and helpers and 159 children] moved off at the appointed time in perfect order, entrained at Vauxhall Station and arrived at their destination at 12.8 p.m.' The destination was Reading. War began two days later, and the raising of the school leaving age, Hadow reorganisation and building grants were for the moment forgotten.

1939 and after

In April 1939 the L.C.C. had issued a four-page pamphlet giving details of the government's scheme 'for the removal of children and certain adults from congested areas should the country be threatened with war'. The scheme was voluntary, and children had to go with the party to which they were attached. The party from St Mark's joined with one from St Stephen's Lambeth at Reading, under the head of St Stephen's. A 'tutorial group' remained at Harleyford Road, but the school could not be brought properly into use without a splinter-proof shelter. A party of senior boys, under a new acting head who had been appointed in 1939 and who returned from Reading for the purpose, met at Henry Fawcett School (one of the nearby L.C.C. schools). The committee were determined that St Mark's should not close, as, they felt in July 1940, 'once closed there was a doubt as to when it would be re-opened'. Two 'refuge rooms' were fitted up in the school, and it was functioning again as a school for the autumn term, with eighty-one children in attendance (and in the meantime Henry Fawcett school had been bombed). In May 1941 part of the premises was in the process of being converted into an air-raid shelter (which involved building a 14 in. wall, reinforcing the cloak-room and protecting windows). It was common early in the war for children gradually to be brought home from evacuation by their parents – though periods of heavy bombing would reverse the trend. By Whitsun 1942 there were 132 children on roll at Harleyford Road, and those in Reading were merged into the host school. The children in London were divided into a class for senior boys, one for senior girls, a junior mixed class and an infant class.

The school therefore remained open throughout the war. In 1943 and 1944 the headmistress recorded continuous air raids and sleepless nights, two incendiary bombs through the roof of the girls' school, lowered attendance when flying bomb attacks began and further evacuations. Slight damage was caused in 1941, but the incendiaries of 1944 put the girls' side of the school out of use, and when it opened at the end of August in that year all the children were accommodated in the boys' classrooms. In 1943 the L.C.C. decided to expand its school meals service, to provide for up to 75 per cent of children on school rolls. It suggested a target of 150 for Kennington, either by building a kitchen or supplying meals from a central kitchen. If the managers were prepared to adopt the former scheme, the L.C.C. would pay for the work and dining equipment, and employ the kitchen staff – a proposal which the managers accepted.

The pre-war beginnings with reorganisation were the basis for war-time proposals for the remodelling of the educational system after the war. The 1944 Education Act was the outcome both of the Hadow momentum and of pressures during the war for a commitment to improvements in social services, social insurance, health and education when the war ended.

In 1938 there had been roughly equal numbers of provided

and non-provided schools in England and Wales (10,363 of the former and 10,553 of the latter), though the provided schools contained over 3 million children and the non-provided under 1½ million. The Church of England accounted for about 9,000 schools, containing a million or so children.[16] Under the Hadow plan and 1936 grant provisions only 519 schemes for new voluntary senior (or secondary) schools had been submitted (well over half for Roman Catholic schools), and only thirty-seven had been built by the outbreak of war.[17] The basis of the 1944 Education Act was the acceptance of the principle of secondary school provision for all over the age of eleven, and the Church of England accepted the need to complete what had been begun. In 1942 the National Society published an *Interim Report on the Dual System*, which declared:[18]

> categorically that it wholly concurs with the intention of His Majesty's Government and the expressed desire of the teaching profession and the general public to secure that the standards of efficiency in primary education shall be raised throughout the country, that the reorganisation of schools for children over 11 shall be completed without delay, and the general school age raised to at least 15 years.

Within the Church there was, however, some resistance. Mr Butler, President of the Board of Education, at a critical meeting with the Archbishop of Canterbury in 1942, made it clear that the Church had no real choice but to concur, whatever hesitations it might have. He read out some very 'damaging statistics' which showed the disparity between provided and non-provided schools:[19]

> He quoted, for example, comparative figures of unreorganised schools, of black listed schools and of schools which had been built in the previous century. The President recorded in his personal memoranda, 'these statistics visibly impressed his Grace who has confirmed to me since that it was on this occasion that he realised that the Government were in earnest about educational reconstruction, and that he would have to do his best to wean his flock from their distaste at the White Memorandum and the alleged threat to their schools.'

As we have seen in the case of Lambeth the voluntary schools were in no position to bargain from strength over the issue of reorganisation, and the 1944 Act embodied various kinds of compromise reached with relatively little acrimony by comparison with 1902.[20] The 1944 Act laid down a strict separation of primary from secondary education, and established three schemes for voluntary schools: special agreement schools (those for which plans had been submitted before the war), voluntary aided and voluntary controlled schools. Controlled schools were to be those whose providing body could not meet its share of the cost of improvements and repairs, and which would virtually be handed to the local authority (while retaining a right to a minority of the membership of the committee of managers, and with certain provision for denominational instruction). Voluntary aided schools would remain under the control of the voluntary body concerned, make their own decisions as to denominational instruction, have two-thirds of the management committee places, and receive in return (apart from the maintenance that had existed since 1902) 50 per cent of approved expenditure on repairs and improvements, and 50 per cent of the cost of alterations made necessary by reorganisation.[21]

While the education bill was before parliament diocesan policy and action were being discussed, and the Kennington school managers registered the fact that the school would 'have no right to appoint teachers unless we can bear 50% of the cost of rebuilding'. The headmistress told the managers 'that what the Church needs are schools for the senior girls and boys, and for those who pass examinations'. It also became clear to them that the voluntary schools would have to pool funds on a diocesan basis, because 'many of the old school sites are not large enough for the size of school, which would have to be rebuilt to meet the required standard of the education authorities'. The decision taken for St Mark's was, in fact, to become a voluntary aided school. When the proposal to become a 'primary mixed' school was discussed by the managers in April 1946, an Assistant Inspector present said that he was anxious that children in Church schools should 'have the same advantage as the children in L.C.C. schools, but unfortunately the Church had not got such a deep pocket as the L.C.C.'.

At the end of the war the school had a roll of some 250 children,

and became a Junior Mixed and Infants' School in 1946. The
reorganisation began in the summer of that year, when all
senior boys were transferred to secondary schools. Two entries
in the headmistress's log book complete the story of reorganisation:

20.12.46　All senior girls transferred to Secondary
　　　　　 Schools . . .
7.1.47　　School reopened as a Junior Mixed and Infants
　　　　　 Dept. with a staff of 2 mistresses for Infants and
　　　　　 4 teachers for Junior Mixed, also a Head Teacher
　　　　　 and a Trainee. Roll 212.

From the following year thirty or so children went on to
secondary schools each summer.

In October 1948 the managers decided to rename the school
the 'St. Mark's, Kennington Oval (J.M. and I)' school, and it
came under district 8 of the L.C.C. Dr Briault, L.C.C. Inspector
for this district (and future Chief Education Officer of the
I.L.E.A.), visited the school for the first time in 1948, and was
present in October 1948 of that year when Miss Hatfield was
appointed headteacher. A permanent headmaster of the boys'
school had not been appointed since the developments of 1937,
and the headmistress was now by definition head of the whole
school. In 1948 the school, which for most of its existence had
been either two separate schools or departments, was now in
every sense a single unit. Miss Hatfield remained head for nine-
teen years, and was succeeded in 1967 by the present headmaster.

When, in 1963, the London Government Act created the
Greater London Council and the L.C.C. disappeared, an Inner
London Education Authority was created for the area formerly
administered by the L.C.C., and St Mark's school came under
division 9 of the new authority early in 1965. In the 1950s
and 1960s consideration was given to 'remodelling' (as the
headmistress described it in 1955) or rebuilding the school on
another site, but it remained physically unchanged – in a
building now listed as of architectural importance. In any
rebuilding plans, therefore, as a school for other purposes, at
least the facade will have to remain.

The staffing and numbers of children in the school in the
post-war period reflected population trends. In the 1950s the
primary schools had to cope with the consequences of the high

birth-rate at the end of the war. In 1955 the headmistress mentions: 'owing to "bulge" difficulties school re-organised into 6 years beginning with entrants. We have been allowed the services of . . . a permanent part-time teacher, to relieve the difficulties in the 5th and 6th years.' By this point, however, the 'bulge' had almost worked its way through the primary schools. What followed can best be followed in the headmistress's log book entries:

3.9.57   Return to school, quite a small intake.
8.1.58   Return to school. Many families seem to be
         moving, the school numbers getting low.
2.9.58   School re-opened, small intake; numbers generally
         in the district have dropped.
26.1.59 Owing to a drop in numbers at the top of the
         school the D.O. (divisional office) have seen fit to
         cut the staff. Re-organisation of the top of the
         school has made it necessary for the head teacher
         to take a class each afternoon – approved by
         H.M.I. – to avoid putting children 'back'.
13.4.59 Return after Easter, numbers improved.

Throughout the 1960s numbers were about 200. The staff authorised for the year 1966–7, for example, were the head-mistress plus 6·5 staff, based on a school roll at that point of 212. In December 1972 the staff consisted of the headmaster and 8·5 teachers (the school now also had a nursery class, with thirty children in the mornings and another thirty in the afternoons).

One of the exciting moments in the life of the school must have been the week in January 1950 when it opened after the holidays, and the headmistress described the arrival of the modern world:

10.1.50 School re-opened to find frontage complete, with
         new notice board, wire fencing, gates and many of
         the rooms wired for electric light.
13.1.50 The first electric switch-on.

In October of the previous year the managers had been pressing the L.C.C. for a plan for the electrification of the school, presented one of their own from a local contractor – which the L.C.C. turned down, and then agreed with the London Electricity Board for the work to be done in the Christmas holidays. The headmistress subsequently wrote in her annual report published in the parish magazine:[22]

> On 13th January we switched on electric light for the first time in the history of the School and even now we cannot believe that it is really true – we often sit in the dark rather than light the 'gas'. Then how much safer the P.T. lessons and playtimes on the new surface of the playground. Also, when we returned after the Christmas holidays we presented a new face to the passing traffic.

More was to follow. The following year she reported the arrival of a wireless set and gramophone pick-up ('and we have used it to the greatest possible advantage ever since').[23] At a meeting of the managers in 1950 the vicar said:

> that he was very anxious to get a sound projector for the use of the school and the church and only a day or two ago had seen one advertised for £150. Two thirds of this sum having been promised, he wondered if the school would like to make up the rest.

The meeting decided to take £50 from the school account for the purpose. An old strip projector was exchanged for a new one in 1963. Also in 1963 the log book mentions that 'television lessons commenced for classes 1 and 2'. In 1967 an H.M.I. visited the school and 'made recommendations re less formal approach in infant department and the possible removal of class 2 to the Art room to enable their present room to be converted into a library and T.V. space'. A kiln and pottery wheel were installed in 1965 and 1966 (when the Rector of Lambeth threw the first pot).

Children were still, in this period, liable to punishment, and teachers open to complaint from parents. Health remained a matter of concern within the school: in 1949, for example, eighty children were immunised against diphtheria 'following serious results of non-immunisation of some children in other districts' – and other immunisation sessions followed. Dental inspections took place, and in 1951 there is the first mention of an audiometer test throughout the school.

One of the most important changes in the educational system was the development of comprehensive schools under the London School Plan of 1947, alongside grammar schools and secondary modern schools. The Kennington records are less indicative of the pattern of secondary education to which its pupils moved, than of the system of selection. In September 1951, for example, the headmistress reported that 'for the first time, a Supplementary Intelligence Test was set – Moray House No. 39', and this became an annual entry in the log book, as well as worthy of mention in the headmistress's annual report for 1951–2 (which indicated some of the schools to which the children went):[24]

> There is now a Supplementary Intelligence Test each year taken as a Preliminary to the Common Entrance Test. This took place on 26th September and the latter on 23rd January. There was yet a further supply of papers for absentees on 12th March. As a result of these tests, one girl is going on to the Charles Edward Brooke Grammar School, one boy to Archbishop Tenison's Grammar School, four girls to Vauxhall Park Central Secondary School, two boys to Archbishop Temple's Central Secondary School, four boys to Hackford Road. The others pass into five Modern Secondary Schools.

Selection on this basis remained the pattern until 1965, when the pressures for the abolition of the eleven-plus nationally, together with the steady increase in the number of London's comprehensive schools, decided the L.C.C. to alter the basis of transfer to secondary schools. It had been concerned 'at the undue influence on the curriculum and methods of the junior schools of the junior leaving examination, which had been part of the transfer procedure'. By 1964 it had seventy-four comprehensive schools, and in that year it decided:[25]

> to introduce a new transfer procedure which embodies two major principles. It does away with the one day junior leaving examination and it no longer places children in 'grammar' or 'non-grammar' categories for transfer purposes. The new scheme of transfer from primary to secondary schools which was introduced in 1965 is designed basically to provide individual guidance and advice to individual children and their parents . . . Central to the procedure is a primary-school profile of the child, which is built up by the primary-school head and staff by means of a cumulative

record of his interests and abilities, attainments and characteristics.

The headmistress of St Mark's attended a meeting in June 1964 'to discuss the transfer to secondary schools in the new system'. In January 1965 she wrote that 'this year is the first of the new "no test" scheme'. Information given to parents by St Mark's school in 1971 explained that:[26]

the 11+ in its original form of tests taken by all London children on the same day at the same time disappeared a few years ago. An important part of the transfer system now in operation is the interview between the child's parents and the Primary School Headteacher . . . Detailed records are kept throughout the child's primary school life . . . From this information and through discussion with the child's teachers and his parents, the Primary School Headteacher makes out a comprehensive report which is passed on to the Secondary School Headteacher.

Information distributed to parents also emphasises, for example, that school journeys and visits are of importance, that sport and swimming are integral parts of the school curriculum, and that all children have to take part in physical education and movement lessons. There is a boys' and girls' school uniform.

It is impossible to discuss here recent changes in the school's curriculum. The school work is summarised for parents in the following way:

The work which children are expected to do, and the way in which it is presented to them, is designed according to the needs and ability of each individual child. Within each class there are children of varying ages and ability and it is not reasonable to expect every child in that class to be at a particular stage of development at the same time. Children within a class are often taught in small groups and some-times as individuals so that each child can benefit to the greatest extent possible.

This summary of the *work* of the school provides one useful terminal point in the story of the school, to be set alongside some of the descriptions of the work in the nineteenth century.

Another terminal point is provided by the following summary
of some of the underlying *purposes* of the school:

> St. Mark's School is smaller than other schools in the area
> and it is not always possible to admit all the children whose
> parents request a place. The School is closely linked with
> St. Mark's Church and preference is given to children whose
> families are linked with the activities of the Church,
> through regular attendance at Church Services or Sunday
> School. School Services are held in the Church about six
> times a year. It is hoped on these occasions that parents
> will join with the School and demonstrate to their children
> that the Christian Church plays an important part in deter-
> mining the outlook which a person has on life. The policy of
> St. Mark's School is that each child should discover his or
> her capabilities and limitations and should be provided with
> a high standard at which to aim but which is well within the
> child's ability to attain. Each child is encouraged to be
> self-disciplined – to behave, speak, dress and work well, not
> because he or she has been told to do so but because these
> are the natural and reasonable things to do for the child's
> own sake and for the sake of others.

Although there are substantial differences between the phrase-
ology and assumptions in this passage and those in parallel
nineteenth-century texts, it is a reminder that the National
Society and the local founders of the Kennington Schools
established a tradition of religious education which is unbroken.
Some indication has been given of those points in their history
when voluntary schools have had greatest difficulties, have
been rescued in one way or another, and brought into a close
relationship with the overall pattern of national legislation and
local provision. This is not the place to assess the profit and loss
of denominational education or the dual system; passages such
as these merely illustrate some of the historical realities behind
what exists.

The school still functions in a social environment which has
come to be called 'under-privileged'. The most profound dis-
tinction between the contemporary primary school and the
monitorial school of 1824, however, is that the discussion is now
about 'each child', not the infant poor. The infant poor still
exist, and the educational system and this school still have to

worry about and provide for them, but they do so within a single structure of public education. This does not mean that all benefit equally within the system: there are fundamental problems still in providing equal educational opportunities for children whose social opportunities are not equal. The primary school is no longer, however, *by definition* for the infant poor.

Notes

Log books of the boys' school, 1908–13, 1913–35, 1935–40.

Log books, girls and infants, 1913–36, 1937–46; junior mixed and infants (1946–   ).

Summary register, 1905–10.

Admission register, girls 1925–   ; boys, girls and infants, 1942–7.

Admission register, boys, 1935–9; juniors and infants, 1947–68.

File of miscellaneous documents, 1937–8.

Committee of Managers, minute book, 1905–53.

1 National Society, St Mark's file; the list is dated 1899.

2 Marjorie Cruikshank, *Church and State in English Education 1870 to the Present Day*, p. 70.

3 Quoted from James C. Greenough, *The Evolution of the Elementary Schools of Great Britain*, pp. 195–9; this reprints the 1902 Act in full.

4 Fabian Society, *The London Education Act 1903; how to make the best of it* (Fabian Tract No. 117), p. 12.

5 L.C.C. Minutes, 30 May 1905, p. 1867 (adjourned Report of the Education Committee).

6 London County Council, Survey and Inspection of Non-Provided Schools. Appendices of Detailed Reports by the Council's Officers, Appendix A – Reports of the Architect (Education) on the School Buildings (April 1905), p. 81. L.C.C. minutes, 30 May 1905, p. 1960 (adjourned Report).

7 National Society, St Mark's file; L.C.C. minutes, 19 June 1907, p. 17 (General Purposes Sub-Committee Report).

8 L.C.C. minutes, 31 January 1905,

p. 227 (Education Committee Report).

9 *Ibid.*, p. 219.

10 L.C.C. minutes, 23 April 1907, p. 1129 (Report of Day Schools Sub-Committee).

11 Flann Campbell, *Eleven-Plus and all that: the grammar school in a changing society*, pp. 71–2. Ch. 4 is a history of scholarships and selection in London.

12 N. Pevsner, *London*, p. 268.

13 For the history of these developments see ch. I ('Sketch of the development of full-time post-primary education in England and Wales from 1800 to 1918'), Board of Education, *The Education of the Adolescent*.

14 *Ibid.*, pp. 172–5.

15 Board of Education, *The New Prospect in Education* (Educational Pamphlet No. 60), pp. 6, 16.

16 Staples' 'Reconstruction' Digests, Education, pt I, *The Spens Report and After*, p. 31.

17 James Murphy, *Church, State and Schools in Britain, 1800–1970*, p. 117.

18 Staples' Digests, *Spens Report and After*, p. 38.
19 Cruikshank, *Church and State in English Education*, pp. 151–2.
20 For a comparison of the acts and situations of 1902 and 1944 see Charmian Cannon, 'The Influence of Religion on Educational Policy, 1902–1944', pp. 143–60.
21 Murphy, *Church, State and Schools in Britain, 1800–1970*, pp. 116–17. By an act of 1959 the building grant was increased to 75 per cent, and in 1966 to 80 per cent. When some semi-major improvements were discussed at Kennington in May 1969, 80 per cent grants were available.
22 *Kennington Chronicle*, August 1950, p. 8.
23 *Ibid.*, August 1951, p. 7.
24 *Ibid.*, August 1952, pp. 7–8.
25 Inner London Education Authority, *London Comprehensive Schools 1966*, p. 24.
26 These and following details are from a dossier of information given to all parents considering registering their children for a place at St Mark's.

Further reading

Chapters 1 and 2

For the economic and social background of the late eighteenth and early nineteenth centuries:

Phyllis Deane, *The First Industrial Revolution* (Cambridge, 1965).
E. J. Hobsbawm, *Industry and Empire: an economic history of Britain since 1750* (London, 1968).

Church and society in the early nineteenth century:

K. S. Inglis, *Churches and the Working Classes in Victorian England* (London, 1963): see Introduction, most of the book covers the later period.
E. R. Wickham, *Church and People in an Industrial City* (London, 1957): a case study of Sheffield.
W. R. Ward, *Religion and Society in England 1790–1850* (London, 1972).

The late-eighteenth-century and early-nineteenth-century background of education and ideas:

Brian Simon, *Studies in the History of Education 1780–1870* (London, 1960): chs I–IV cover this period.
Harold Silver, *The Concept of Popular Education: a study of ideas and social movements in the early nineteenth century* (London, 1965).

The National Society:

Henry James Burgess, *Enterprise in Education: the story of the work of the Established Church in the education of the people prior to 1870* (London, 1958).

Monitorial education:

Charles Birchenough, *History of Elementary Education in England and Wales from 1800 to the Present Day* (London, 3rd edn 1938): chs II and IX.
Mary Sturt, *The Education of the People: a history of primary education in England and Wales in the nineteenth century* (London, 1967): ch. 2.

Radical educational views and experiments:

Brian Simon, see above.
W. A. C. Stewart and W. P. McCann, *The Educational Innovators
1750–1880* (London, 1967): chs I–V.

For the early history of Lambeth, the most useful are the relevant
volumes of the Survey of London (for details, see the Bibliography,
section (iii)).

Chapter 3

General school conditions:

Mary Sturt, *The Education of the People*, chs 1–6.

Teachers:

R. W. Rich, *The Training of Teachers in England and Wales during
the Nineteenth Century* (Cambridge, 1933), chs I and II.

Infant schools:

Nanette Whitbread, *The Evolution of the Nursery-Infant School: a
history of infant and nursery education in Britain, 1800–1970*
(London, 1972), ch. 1.

Chapter 4

The development of educational administration and controversy at
this period and later in the century:

J. J. and A. J. Bagley, *The State and Education in England and Wales
1833–1968* (London, 1969).
Gillian Sutherland, *Elementary Education in the Nineteenth Century*
(London, 1971): a Historical Association pamphlet.

Pupil teachers and the 1846 reforms:

Asher Tropp, *The School Teachers: the growth of the teaching profession
in England and Wales from 1800 to the present day* (London, 1957):
chs II and III.
R. W. Rich, *The Training of Teachers*, chs III–VI.

School architecture and design in this period and at other times in the
nineteenth century:

Malcolm Seaborne, *The English School: its architecture and organization
1370–1870* (London, 1971): chs 8–10 and illustrations.

Chapter 5

Urban conditions in the middle of the nineteenth century:

Norman Longmate, *King Cholera: the biography of a disease* (London, 1966): an excellent introduction to the specific problems discussed in this chapter, and the wider social background.

J. L. and Barbara Hammond, *The Age of the Chartists 1832–1854: a study of discontent* (London, 1930): still a good account of towns, education, religion, health . . . in this period.

Chapter 6

The Newcastle Commission, the Revised Code and payment by results:
Mary Sturt, *The Education of the People:* chs 13–14.

Chapter 7

Many of the suggestions for earlier chapters also cover this period of the nineteenth century. In addition:

The general background of education and educational ideas, 1870–1900:

Brian Simon, *Education and the Labour Movement 1870–1920* (London, 1965): especially chs III and IV.

London education, the School Board, poverty and attendance:

David Rubinstein, *School Attendance in London 1870–1904: a social history* (Hull, 1969).

The urban background of the second half of the nineteenth century, including London:

Asa Briggs, *Victorian Cities* (London, 1963).

On Lambeth, in addition to the Survey of London volumes, there is the flimsy but useful for this period:

Aileen Denise Nash, *Living in Lambeth 1086–1914* (undated [1951]).

The Church of England and education:

Marjorie Cruikshank, *Church and State in English Education 1870 to the Present Day* (London, 1964); especially ch. 3.

Teachers: in addition to the relevant chapters in Tropp there is:

Richard Bourne and Brian Macarthur, *The Struggle for Education 1870–1970: a pictorial history of popular education and the National Union of Teachers* (London, undated [1970]).

Chapter 8

Twentieth-century English education in general:

Gerald Bernbaum, *Social Change and the Schools 1918–1944* (London, 1967).

H. C. Dent, *The Educational System of England and Wales* (London, 1960; and later edns): for brief historical and administrative explanations of some of the organisational developments discussed here.

R. D. Bramwell, *Elementary School Work 1900–1925* (Durham, 1961): mainly the elementary school curriculum.

Board of Education, *The Education of the Adolescent* (Hadow Report, London, 1927): ch. I for historical sketch of development of post-primary education, ch. II the facts of the situation in the 1920s, and remainder for reorganisation proposals.

Board of Education, *The Primary School* (2nd Hadow Report, London, 1931); ch. I for history of primary education.

Education, religion, voluntary schools:

Marjorie Cruikshank, *Church and State in English Education 1870 to the Present Day.*

Murphy, James, *Church, State and Schools in Britain, 1800–1970* (London, 1971).

Both of the above contain chapters on 1902, 1944 and other aspects. In addition, on 1902:

E. J. R. Eaglesham, *The Foundations of 20th Century Education in England* (London, 1967).

And on 1944:

H. C. Dent, *The Education Act, 1944* (London, 1944; and later edns).

A. G. Wedderspoon (ed.), *Religious Education 1944–84* (London, 1966): especially article by W. Roy Niblett, 'The Religious Clauses of the 1944 Act'.

For the Second World War:

H. C. Dent, *Education in Transition: a sociological study of the impact of war on English education 1939–1943* (London, 1944).

For the scholarship 'ladder':

Flann Campbell, *Eleven Plus and All That: the grammar school in a changing society* (London, 1956): ch. 4, 'Scholarships and methods of selection'.

Olive Banks, *Parity and Prestige in English Secondary Education* (London, 1955): particularly chs. 4, 'The higher elementary schools' and 5, 'The free place regulations'. Also chs on higher-grade schools, central schools, secondary education for all.

N

New ideas in elementary education in 1920s and 1930s:

R. J. W. Selleck, *English Primary Education and the Progressives,
1914–1939* (London, 1972).

Child health and welfare:

Ministry of Education, *Report of the Committee on Maladjusted
Children* (Underwood Report, London, 1955): ch. II—a useful
historical background to child psychology.

W. Penelope Hall, *The Social Services of Modern England* (London,
1952; and later edns): ch. XII, 'The health and welfare of the school
child', provides brief historical information.

London County Council:

W. Eric Jackson, *Achievement: a short history of the London County
Council* (London, 1965): chs include housing and education.

General

In addition to the suggestions at the end of each chapter, the following
are some books of general interest.

Histories of schools and local education:

Malcolm Seaborne, *Recent Education from Local Sources* (London,
1967): a study of education in Leicester.

Rex C. Russell, *A History of Schools and Education in Lindsey,
Lincolnshire 1800–1902* (Lindsey, 1965–7): four pamphlets, on the
foundation and maintenance of schools for the poor, Sunday
Schools, the Church of England and elementary education,
methodism and day schools.

Elizabeth Raistrick, *Village Schools: an Upper Wharfedale history*
(Clapham (via Lancaster), 1971).

John Lawson, *A Town Grammar School through Six Centuries: a history
of Hull Grammar School against its local background* (London, 1963):
a model history of a grammar school.

David Wardle, *Education and Society in Nineteenth-Century Nottingham*
(Cambridge, 1971): ch. 4 is on 'the work of the voluntary schools'.

Sources, and the use of them:

R. B. Pugh, 'Sources for the History of English Primary Schools',
British Journal of Educational Studies, I (1952–3).

W. B. Stephens, *Sources for English Local History* (Manchester, 1973):
ch. VII—'Education'.

The history of education:

Stuart Maclure, *One Hundred Years of London Education 1870–1970*
(London, 1970): for the background to the later period covered in
this book.

John Lawson and Harold Silver, *A Social History of Education in England* (London, 1973).

J. Stuart Maclure, *Educational Documents England and Wales, 1816–1963* (London, 1965): a useful reference work for explanations of the main reports and legislation.

J. J. and A. J. Bagley, *The State and Education in England and Wales 1833–1968*: a simple introduction to the administrative history.

Bibliography

(i) *Manuscript records in the possession of St Mark's School, Kennington*

Bound volume of minutes and various documents 1823–40
Amount of collections at St Mark's Church, Kennington, for the District Charity Schools, 1826–43 (double sheet)
Papers relating to drainage: applications to the Commissioners of Sewers, 1849–54
Subscriptions and donations book 1853–4
Minute book and correspondence 1854–6
Visitors' book, 1854–64
File of miscellaneous documents relating to St Mark's School in the mid-nineteenth century
Book containing items requiring Committee approval, 1863–95
Master's and mistress' report book 1863–95
File of duplicate examination schedules and inspectors' reports, 1879–1905
General registers of the Science School, Kennington Oval School, 1879–88, 1888–91 (tied together)
Applications for Headmistress, Oval Schools, Xmas 1889 (double sheet)
Regency Square Schools, Minute book, 1852–60
Receipts and expenses, 1824–46
Account book, 1854–1901
Treasurer's accounts, 1883–93
Account book, 1913–36
Cash books, 1868–87; 1874–80; 1881–7; 1887–1893; 1893–7; 1926–31
Folders of cheques, 1931–2, 1935
Envelope containing cheques and cheque particulars, 1934
Postage book, 1934–48
File of miscellaneous documents, 1937–8
Bank paying-in books (meals), 1945–50 (6 books)
School meals account book, 1948–50
Dinner book, 1949
Envelope of receipts, 1932
Envelope of wear and tear statements, 1934
Envelope of fire insurance papers, 1934–5
Envelope of accounts relating to floor, 1935
Envelope of rating valuations and other documents, 1933–8
Envelope of miscellaneous documents, 1935

Envelope of miscellaneous documents, 1935–6
Envelope of insurance policies
General stock and stores book, 1904–9
Envelope containing copy of history of St Mark's School for *Survey of London*
Log books, girls, 1862–71; 1871–99; 1899–1913
Log book, girls and infants, 1913–36
Log book, infants, 1884–1907
Log books, boys, 1863–80; 1895–1908; 1908–13; 1913–35; 1935–40
Admission registers, girls, 1881–1900; 1900–25; 1925– ; boys, girls and infants, 1942–7
Admission registers, infants, 1889–1907; 1907–27; 1927–39
Admission register, boys, 1874–82
Admission registers (loose pages only), boys, 1882–8; 1888–1900
Admission register, boys, 1935–9; juniors and infants, 1947–68
Applications for admission book, 1906–7
Summary registers, 1875–7; 1878–80; 1880–5; 1890–4; 1895–1900; 1900–5; 1905–10
Committee of Managers, minute book, 1905–53
St Mark's School Kennington, Information (booklet prepared for parents)

(ii) *Other manuscript and primary sources*

Burgess, H. J., 'The Educational History of the National Society 1811–1833' (unpublished London University M.A. thesis, 1949).
Census, 1841 and 1851, Lambeth returns.
Census, 1851, Ecclesiastical returns.
Charity Commissioners, *Report on Endowed Charities* (County of London), 1901–3, vol. IV.
Clowes, Rollo Laird, 'History of the Manor of Kennington in the County of Surrey' (unpublished manuscript bound in four volumes, 1916, Minet Library, Brixton).
Committee of Council on Education, *Minutes*, 1840/1–6; *Report*, 1868–9.
General Board of Health, *Notification*, 20 September 1853; *Precautionary Advice to Local Boards with reference to Cholera*, 15 September 1853.
Lewis, Pamela C., 'The Early Charity Schools and National Schools of Tooting and Streatham' (unpublished essay, Furzedown Training College, 1950, Minet Library, Brixton).
London County Council, Minutes.
London County Council Education Committee, Minutes.
London County Council Official Publications, vol. 74.
National Society, *Annual Reports*, 1812–45.
National Society, St Mark's file.
Rothley National School, Leicestershire, log book, 1872–1907.
Society for the Encouragement of Parochial Schools in the Diocese of Durham and Hexhamshire, *Annual Reports*, 1812–24.

(iii) *Secondary sources*

Adams, Francis, *History of the Elementary School Contest in England* (London, 1882).

Allen, J. T., *A Vindication of the Moral and Religious Instruction of the Children of the Poor* (Manchester, 1820).

Allen, Thomas, *The History and Antiquities of the Parish of Lambeth* (London, 1826).

Altick, Richard D., *The English Common Reader: a social history of the mass reading public 1800–1900* (Chicago, 1957).

Archer, R. L., *Secondary Education in the Nineteenth Century* (London, 1921; 1966 edn).

Bartley, George C. T., *The Schools for the People, containing the history, development, and present working of each description of English school for the industrial and poorer classes* (London, 1871).

Bell, Andrew, *The Madras School* (London, 1808).

Bernard, Thomas, *The Barrington School* (London, 1812).

Birchenough, Charles, *History of Elementary Education in England and Wales from 1800 to the Present Day* (London, 1927; 1938 3rd edn).

Board of Education, *The Education of the Adolescent* (Hadow Report, London, 1927).

Board of Education, *The New Prospect in Education* (Educational Pamphlet no. 60, London, 1928).

Burgess, H. J., *Enterprise in Education: the story of the work of the established church in the education of the people prior to 1870* (London, 1958).

Burgess, H. J. and Welsby, P. A., *A Short History of the National Society 1811–1961* (London, 1961).

Campbell, Flann, *Eleven-Plus and all that: the grammar school in a changing society* (London, 1956).

Cannon, Charmian, 'The Influence of Religion on Educational Policy, 1902–1944', *British Journal of Educational Studies*, XII (1963–4).

Carrington, R. C., *Two Schools: a history of the St. Olave's and St. Saviour's Grammar School Foundation* (London, 1971).

Christian, G. A., *English Education from Within* (London, 1922).

Cruikshank, Marjorie, *Church and State in English Education 1870 to the Present Day* (London, 1964).

Davies, E. T., *Monmouthshire Schools and Education to 1870* (Newport, 1957).

Dobbs, A. E., *Education and Social Movements 1700–1850* (London, 1919).

Eades, G. E., *Historic London* (London, 1966).

Fabian Society, *The London Education Act 1903: how to make the best of it* (Fabian Tract No. 117, London, 1904).

Gomme, G. Lawrence, *London in the Reign of Victoria* (London, 1898).

Greenough, James C., *The Evolution of the Elementary Schools of Great Britain* (New York, 1903).

Inner London Education Authority, *London Comprehensive Schools 1966* (London, 1967).

Johnson, Marion, *Derbyshire Village Schools in the Nineteenth Century* (Newton Abbot, 1970).

Kay-Shuttleworth, James, *The School in its Relations to the State, the Church, and the Congregation, being an explanation of the Minutes of the Committee of Council on Education* (London, 1847).

Kennington Chronicle, 1950–2.

Lancaster, Joseph, *An Appeal for Justice in the Cause of Ten Thousand Poor Children* (London, 1806).

Lancaster, Joseph, *Improvements in Education* (London, 1806).

Longmate, Norman, *King Cholera: the biography of a disease* (London, 1966).

Maclure, Stuart, *One Hundred Years of London Education 1870–1970* (London, 1970).

Mann, Horace, *Census of Great Britain, 1851: Education in Great Britain* (London, 1854).

Manning, O. and Bray, W., *The History and Antiquities of the County of Surrey* (London, 1804–14), 3 vols.

Montgomery, H. H., *The History of Kennington and its Neighbourhood* (London, 1889).

Murphy, James, *Church, State and Schools in Britain, 1800–1970* (London, 1971).

Nash, Aileen Denise, *Living in Lambeth 1086–1914* (London, undated [1951]).

Pevsner, Nikolaus, *The Buildings of England: London* (Harmondsworth, 1952).

Ragged School Union, 'The London Ragged Schools', *Occasional Paper No. III* (London, 1847).

Rich, R. W., *The Training of Teachers in England and Wales during the Nineteenth Century* (Cambridge, 1933).

Roberts, A. F. B., 'A New View of the Infant School Movement', *British Journal of Educational Studies*, xx (1972).

Royal Commission on the Distribution of the Industrial Population, *Minutes of Evidence* (Barlow Report, London, 1940).

Rubinstein, David, *School Attendance in London, 1870–1904: a social history* (Hull, 1969).

Russell, Rex C., *A History of Schools and Education in Lindsey, Lincolnshire 1800–1902* (Lindsey, 1965–7). Pt one – *The Foundation and Maintenance of Schools for the Poor;* pt three – *The Church of England and the Provision of Elementary Education.*

Sadler, M. E. and Edwards, J. W., 'Public Elementary Education in England and Wales, 1870–1895', *Special Reports on Educational Subjects 1896–7* (London, 1897).

Sadler, M. E. and Edwards, J. W., 'Summary of Statistics, Regulations, &c., of Elementary Education in England and Wales. 1833–1870', *Special Reports on Educational Subjects*, II (London, 1898).

Sandford, Francis (ed.), *Reports on Elementary Schools 1852–1882 by Matthew Arnold* (London, 1889).

Schools Enquiry Commission, *Report* (Bryce Commission, London, 1895).

Selleck, R. J. W., *English Primary Education and the Progressives, 1914–1939* (London, 1972).

Silver, Harold, *The Concept of Popular Education: a study of ideas and social movements in the early nineteenth century* (London, 1965).

Simon, Brian, *Studies in the History of Education 1780–1870* (London, 1960).

Simon, Brian, *Education and the Labour Movement 1870–1920* (London, 1965).

Smith, Frank, *A History of English Elementary Education 1760–1902* (London, 1931).

Society for Bettering the Condition of the Poor, *Of the Education of the Poor; being the first part of a digest of the reports of the Society . . .* (London, 1809).

Staples, 'Reconstruction' Digests, Education, pt I, *The Spens Report and After* (London, 1943).

Stone, Lawrence, 'Literacy and Education in England 1640–1900', *Past and Present*, no. 42 (1969).

Sturt, Mary, *The Education of the People: a history of primary education in England and Wales in the nineteenth century* (London, 1967).

Survey of London, XXIII, *South Bank and Vauxhall*, pt I (London, 1951).

Survey of London, XXVI, *The Parish of St. Mary Lambeth*, pt II (London, 1956).

Szreter, R., 'The Origins of Full-time Compulsory Education at Five', *British Journal of Educational Studies*, XIII (1964).

Tanswell, John, *The History and Antiquities of Lambeth* (London, 1858).

Tropp, Asher, *The School Teachers: the growth of the teaching profession in England and Wales from 1800 to the present day* (London, 1957).

Victoria History of the County of Surrey, IV (London, 1912; 1967 edn).

Weber, Adna Ferrin, *The Growth of Cities in the Nineteenth Century* (New York, 1899; 1963 edn).

Index